LONDON
WINE BARS GUIDE
2020
Recommended for Tourists
The Top-Rated Wine Bars In The City

THE ULTIMATE LIST OF THE BEST WINE BARS ACCORDING TO VISITORS

LONDON WINE BARS GUIDE 2020
The Top-Rated Wine Bars In The City Of London

© Martin G. McEwan, 2020
© E.G.P. Editorial, 2020

Printed in USA.

ISBN-13: 9781082262722

LONDON WINE BARS GUIDE 2020

Listing The Top-Rated Wine Bars In The City

This book is dedicated to the Owners and Managers who provide the experience
that the locals and tourists enjoy. Thanks you very much for all that you do
and thank for being the "People Choice".

Thanks to everyone that posts their reviews online and
the amazing reviews sites that make our life easier.

The places listed in this book are the most positively reviewed
and recommended by locals and travelers from around the world.

Thank you for your time and enjoy the book that is
designed with locals and tourist in mind!

TOP 500
WINE BARS

The Most Recommended

(from #1 to #500)

#1
Gordon's Wine Bar
Cuisines: Wine Bar, Lounge
Average price: Modest
Area: Strand
Address: 47 Villiers Street
London WC2N 6NE
Phone: 020 7930 1408

#2
Cork & Bottle
Cuisines: Wine Bar
Average price: Modest
Area: Leicester Square
Address: 44-46 Cranbourn Street
London WC2H 7AN
Phone: 020 7734 6592

#3
The Remedy
Cuisines: Wine Bar, European
Average price: Modest
Area: Fitzrovia
Address: 124 Cleveland Street
London W1T 6PG
Phone: 020 3489 3800

#4
Le Beaujolais
Cuisines: Wine Bar, French
Average price: Expensive
Area: Covent Garden
Address: 25 Litchfield Street
London WC2H 9NJ
Phone: 020 7836 2955

#5
Sager + Wilde - Hackney Road
Cuisines: Wine Bar, Tapas
Average price: Expensive
Area: Shoreditch, Haggerston
Address: 193 Hackney Road
London E2 8JL
Phone: 020 8127 7330

#6
Vagabond Wines
Cuisines: Wine Bar, Beer,
Wine & Spirits
Average price: Modest
Area: Fitzrovia
Address: 25 Charlotte Street
London W1T 1RW
Phone: 020 3441 9210

#7
Vinoteca
Cuisines: Wine Bar, European
Average price: Expensive
Area: Marylebone
Address: 15 Seymour Place
London W1H 5BD
Phone: 020 7724 7288

#8
28-50 Wine Workshop and Kitchen
Cuisines: Wine Bar, European
Average price: Expensive
Area: Marylebone
Address: 15-17 Marylebone Lane
London W1U 2NE
Phone: 020 7486 7922

#9
The Sampler
Cuisines: Beer, Wine & Spirits, Venue
& Event Space, Wine Bar
Average price: Modest
Area: South Kensington
Address: 35 Thurloe Place
London SW7 2HP
Phone: 020 7225 5091

#10
Negozio Classica
Cuisines: Italian, Wine Bar
Average price: Modest
Area: Notting Hill
Address: 283 Westbourne Grove
London W11 2QA
Phone: 020 7034 0005

#11
Noble Rot Wine Bar
Cuisines: Wine Bar
Average price: Expensive
Area: Bloomsbury
Address: 51 Lamb's Conduit Street
London WC1N 3NG
Phone: 020 7242 8963

#12
Lanesborough Hotel Library Bar
Cuisines: Wine Bar, Lounge
Average price: Expensive
Area: Belgravia
Address: Lanesborough Place
London SW1X 7TA
Phone: 020 7259 5599

#13
Ain't Nothin' But...
Cuisines: Jazz & Blues,
Dance Club, Wine Bar
Average price: Modest
Area: Soho
Address: 20 Kingly Street
London W1B 5PZ
Phone: 020 7287 0514

#14
The Sampler
Cuisines: Beer, Wine & Spirits,
Wine Bar
Average price: Expensive
Area: Islington
Address: 266 Upper Street
London N1 2UQ
Phone: 020 7226 9500

#15
Vagabond Wines
Cuisines: Wine Bar
Average price: Modest
Area: Spitalfields
Address: 67 Brushfield Street
London E1 6AA
Phone: 020 3674 5670

#16
Boot and Flogger
Cuisines: Wine Bar, British
Average price: Modest
Area: Borough
Address: 10-20 Redcross Way
London SE1 1TA
Phone: 020 7407 1116

#17
Terroirs
Cuisines: Wine Bar, French
Average price: Expensive
Area: Covent Garden, Strand
Address: 5 William IV Street
London WC2N 4DW
Phone: 020 7036 0660

#18
Vini Italiani
Cuisines: Wine Bar
Average price: Modest
Area: South Kensington
Address: 72 Old Brompton Road
London SW7 3LQ
Phone: 020 7225 2283

#19
Vinoteca
Cuisines: Wine Bar, European
Average price: Modest
Area: Farringdon
Address: 7 St John Street
London EC1M 4AA
Phone: 020 7253 8786

#20
Salt Yard
Cuisines: Tapas Bar, Wine Bar
Average price: Expensive
Area: Fitzrovia
Address: 54 Goodge Street
London W1T 4NA
Phone: 020 7637 0657

#21
The Providores and Tapa Room
Cuisines: European, Wine Bar,
Breakfast & Brunch
Average price: Modest
Area: Marylebone
Address: 109 Marylebone High Street
London W1U 4RX
Phone: 020 7935 6175

#22
Vinoteca
Cuisines: Wine Bar, European
Average price: Expensive
Area: Soho
Address: 53-55 Beak Street
London W1F 9SH
Phone: 020 3544 7411

#23
Meson Don Felipe
Cuisines: Wine Bar, Spanish, Basque
Average price: Modest
Area: Southwark, Waterloo
Address: 53 The Cut
London SE1 8LF
Phone: 020 7928 3237

#24
The Ebury Restaurant and Wine Bar
Cuisines: Wine Bar, British, Vegetarian
Average price: Modest
Area: Belgravia
Address: 139 Ebury Street
London SW1W 9QU
Phone: 020 7730 5447

#25
The Fulham Wine Rooms
Cuisines: Wine Bar, European,
Tapas Bar
Average price: Expensive
Area: Fulham, Parsons Green
Address: 871-873 Fulham Road
London SW6 5HP
Phone: 020 7042 9440

#26
Chez Elles
Cuisines: French, Wine Bar
Average price: Modest
Area: Brick Lane, Shoreditch
Address: 45 Brick Lane
London E1 6PU
Phone: 020 7247 9699

#27
Cecconi's
Cuisines: Italian, Wine Bar
Average price: Expensive
Area: Mayfair
Address: 5-5A Burlington Gardens
London W1S 3EP
Phone: 020 7434 1500

#28
The Vineyard
Cuisines: Wine Bar
Average price: Modest
Area: Islington
Address: 179 Upper Street
London N1 1RG
Phone: 020 7226 6276

#29
Bar Du Marché
Cuisines: Wine Bar, French
Average price: Modest
Area: Soho
Address: 19 Berwick Street
London W1F 0PX
Phone: 020 7734 4606

#30
The Northall
Cuisines: Wine Bar, British
Average price: Expensive
Area: Westminster
Address: 10a Northumberland Avenue
London WC2N 5AE
Phone: 020 7321 3100

#31
Tbilisi
Cuisines: Wine Bar, Georgian
Average price: Modest
Area: Lower Holloway
Address: 91 Holloway Road
London N7 8LT
Phone: 020 7607 2536

#33
28-50
Cuisines: Wine Bar, French
Average price: Expensive
Area: Holborn
Address: 140 Fetter Lane
London EC4A 1BT
Phone: 020 7242 8877

#32
The Wells
Cuisines: Wine Bar, Pub, British
Average price: Modest
Area: Hampstead Village
Address: 30 Well Walk
London NW3 1BX
Phone: 020 7794 3785

#34
Vinoteca Kings Cross
Cuisines: Wine Bar, Beer, Wine &
Spirits, European
Average price: Modest
Area: King's Cross
Address: One Pancras Square
London N1C 4AG
Phone: 020 3793 7210

#35
Wine Rooms
Cuisines: Tapas Bar, Wine Bar,
European
Average price: Modest
Area: Notting Hill
Address: 127-129 Kensington Church
Street, London W8 7LP
Phone: 020 7727 8142

#36
The Port House
Cuisines: Tapas, Wine Bar
Average price: Modest
Area: Covent Garden, Strand
Address: 417 Strand
London WC2R 0PD
Phone: 020 7836 7764

#37
Bar Américain
Cuisines: Wine Bar, Cocktail Bar,
Champagne Bar
Average price: Modest
Area: Soho
Address: 20 Sherwood Street
London W1F 7ED
Phone: 020 7734 4888

#38
Tuscanic
Cuisines: Italian, Wine Bar
Average price: Modest
Area: Soho
Address: 72 Old Compton Street
London W1D 4UN
Phone: 020 3659 9243

#39
Bedford & Strand
Cuisines: Wine Bar, European,
Venue & Event Space
Average price: Modest
Area: Covent Garden, Strand
Address: 1a Bedford Street
London WC2E 9HH
Phone: 020 7836 3033

#40
Bedales of Borough Market
Cuisines: Beer, Wine & Spirits,
Wine Bar, Tapas
Average price: Modest
Area: London Bridge
Address: 5 Bedale Street
London SE1 9AL
Phone: 020 7403 8853

#41
Shampers
Cuisines: French, Wine Bar
Average price: Modest
Area: Soho
Address: 4 Kingly Street
London W1B 5PE
Phone: 020 7437 1692

#42
Ashbee's Wine Bars
Cuisines: Wine Bar
Average price: Expensive
Area: South Kensington
Address: 22-24 Hogarth Place
London SW5 0QY
Phone: 020 7373 6180

#43
Cotto
Cuisines: Italian, Wine Bar
Average price: Modest
Area: Southwark, Vauxhall
Address: 89 Westminster Bridge Road
London SE1 7HR
Phone: 020 7928 5535

#44
Village East
Cuisines: Wine Bar, European, British
Average price: Expensive
Area: Borough
Address: 171-173 Bermondsey Street
London SE1 3UW
Phone: 020 7357 6082

#45
Planet of the Grapes
Cuisines: Wine Bar, British, Beer,
Wine & Spirits
Average price: Expensive
Area: The City
Address: 74-82 Queen Victoria Street
London EC4N 4SJ
Phone: 020 7248 1892

#46
Champagne Charlies
Cuisines: Wine Bar, British
Average price: Modest
Area: Strand
Address: 17 The Arches
London WC2N 6NG
Phone: 020 7930 7737

#47
Vivat Bacchus
Cuisines: European, Wine Bar
Average price: Modest
Area: Farringdon
Address: 47 Farringdon Street
London EC4A 4LL
Phone: 020 7353 2648

#48
Notes
Cuisines: Coffee & Tea,
Patisserie/Cake Shop, Wine Bar
Average price: Modest
Area: Covent Garden, Strand
Address: 31 St Martin's Lane
London WC2N 4ER
Phone: 020 7240 0424

#49
Coco Momo
Cuisines: Wine Bar, American
Average price: Modest
Area: Marylebone
Address: 79 Marylebone High Street
London W1U 5JZ
Phone: 020 7486 5746

#50
Notes Kings Cross
Cuisines: Coffee & Tea, Wine Bar
Average price: Modest
Area: King's Cross
Address: One Pancras Square
London N1C 4AG
Phone: 020 3479 1576

#51
40 Maltby Street
Cuisines: Wine Bar
Average price: Modest
Area: Borough
Address: 40 Maltby Street
London SE1 3PA
Phone: 020 7237 9247

#52
Villiers
Cuisines: British, Cafe, Wine Bar
Average price: Modest
Area: Strand
Address: 31A Villiers Street
London WC2N 6ND
Phone: 020 7925 2100

#53
Le Vieux Comptoir
Cuisines: French, Wine Bar,
Cheese Shop
Average price: Modest
Area: Marylebone
Address: 20 Moxon Street
London W1U 4EU
Phone: 020 7224 0303

#54
Smithy's
Cuisines: Wine Bar
Average price: Modest
Area: Bloomsbury
Address: 15-17 Leeke Street
London WC1X 9HY
Phone: 020 7278 5949

#55
Enoteca Rabezzana
Cuisines: Wine Bar, Italian
Average price: Modest
Area: Farringdon
Address: 62-63 Long Lane
London EC1A 9EJ
Phone: 020 7600 0266

#56
Crusting Pipe
Cuisines: Wine Bar
Average price: Modest
Area: Covent Garden, Strand
Address: 27 Covent Garden Market
London WC2E 8RD
Phone: 020 7836 1415

#57
Tapas Brindisa
Cuisines: Tapas Bar, Wine Bar,
Breakfast & Brunch
Average price: Modest
Area: London Bridge
Address: 18-20 Southwark Street
London SE1 1TJ
Phone: 020 7357 8880

#58
Amuse Bouche
Cuisines: Wine Bar, Champagne Bar
Average price: Expensive
Area: Soho
Address: 21-22 Poland Street
London W1F 8QG
Phone: 020 7287 1661

#59
1707 Wine Bar
Cuisines: Wine Bar
Average price: Inexpensive
Area: Mayfair
Address: 118 Piccadilly
London W1A 1ER
Phone: 0845 602 5694

#60
Cafe El Buen Gusto
Cuisines: Mediterranean, Wine Bar,
Tapas Bar
Average price: Modest
Area: Bloomsbury
Address: 39 Frith Street
London W1D 5LL
Phone: 020 7159 4440

#61
The Wine Parlour
Cuisines: Wine Bar
Average price: Modest
Area: Coldharbour Lane/ Herne Hill
Address: 1 & 3 Vining Street
London SW9 8QA
Phone: 020 3302 1617

#62
Le Metro
Cuisines: Wine Bar, Bistros,
Tea Room
Average price: Modest
Area: Chelsea
Address: 28 Basil Street
London SW3 1AS
Phone: 020 7589 6286

#63
Blackfriars Wine Bar Warehouse
Cuisines: Wine Bar
Average price: Modest
Area: Southwark
Address: Arch 80 Scoresby Street
London SE1 0XN
Phone: 020 7928 0905

#64
The Artisan Bistro
Cuisines: Wine Bar, Bistros,
Mediterranean
Average price: Expensive
Area: South Kensington
Address: 14 Hollywood Road
London SW10 9HY
Phone: 020 7460 0875

#65
Bedales at Spitalfields Market
Cuisines: Wine Bar, Wine & Spirits
Average price: Modest
Area: Spitalfields
Address: 12 Market Street
London E1 6DT
Phone: 020 7375 1926

#66
Humble Grape
Cuisines: Wine Bar
Average price: Modest
Area: Clapham, Clapham Common,
Clapham Junction
Address: 2 Battersea Rise
London SW11 1ED
Phone: 020 3620 2202

#67
The Den
Cuisines: Wine Bar, Cocktail Bar
Average price: Modest
Area: Soho
Address: 100 Wardour Street
London W1F 0TN
Phone: 020 7314 4090

#68
The Lonsdale
Cuisines: Wine Bar, Lounge, American
Average price: Expensive
Area: Notting Hill
Address: 48 Lonsdale Road
London W11 2DE
Phone: 020 7727 4080

#69
Pall Mall Fine Wine
Cuisines: Wine Bar, Lounge
Average price: Modest
Area: St James's
Address: 6 & 7 Royal Opera Arcade
London SW1Y 4UY
Phone: 020 7321 2529

#70
Soif
Cuisines: Wine Bar, British, French
Average price: Expensive
Area: Clapham Junction
Address: 27 Battersea Rise
London SW11 1HG
Phone: 020 7223 1112

#71
Portland
Cuisines: Wine Bar, British
Average price: Exclusive
Area: Fitzrovia
Address: 113 Great Portland Street
London W1W 6QQ
Phone: 020 7436 3261

#72
Le QuecumBar & Brasserie
Cuisines: Wine Bar, Brasserie
Average price: Expensive
Area: Battersea
Address: 42-44 Battersea High Street
London SW11 3HX
Phone: 020 7787 2227

#73
Arches Wine Bar
Cuisines: Wine Bar
Average price: Modest
Area: West Hampstead
Address: 7 Fairhazel Gardens
London NW6 3QE
Phone: 020 7624 1867

#74
The Refinery
Cuisines: Wine Bar, British
Average price: Modest
Area: Southwark
Address: 110 Southwark Street
London SE1 0TF
Phone: 0845 468 0186

#75
Drake's Tabanco
Cuisines: Wine Bar
Average price: Modest
Area: Fitzrovia
Address: 3 Windmill Street
London W1T 2HY
Phone: 020 7637 9388

#76
Compagnie des Vins Surnaturels
Cuisines: French, Wine Bar
Average price: Expensive
Area: Covent Garden
Address: 8-10 Neal's Yard
London WC2H 9DP
Phone: 020 7734 7737

#77
Enoteca Supertuscan
Cuisines: Wine Bar
Average price: Modest
Area: Aldgate
Address: 8A Artillery Passage
London E1 7LJ
Phone: 020 7247 8717

#78
Mark's Bar at Hix
Cuisines: Wine Bar, Cocktail Bar
Average price: Expensive
Area: Soho
Address: 66-70 Brewer Street
London W1F 9UP
Phone: 020 7292 3518

#79
Planet Of The Grapes
Cuisines: Wine Bar
Average price: Modest
Area: Aldgate
Address: 9 Bulls Head Passage
London EC3V 1LU
Phone: 020 7929 7224

#80
The Bok Bar
Cuisines: Pub, Thai, Wine Bar
Average price: Modest
Area: Marylebone
Address: 56 Blandford Street
London W1U 7JA
Phone: 020 7467 3820

#81
IDDU
Cuisines: Wine Bar, Italian,
Cocktail Bar
Average price: Modest
Area: South Kensington
Address: 44 Harrington Road
London SW7 3ND
Phone: 020 7589 1991

#82
The Folly
Cuisines: Wine Bar, European
Average price: Modest
Area: The City
Address: 41 Gracechurch Street
London EC3V 0BT
Phone: 0845 468 0102

#83
Chairs and Coffee
Cuisines: Coffee & Tea, Wine Bar
Average price: Inexpensive
Area: Fulham
Address: 512 Fulham Road
London SW6 5NJ
Phone: 020 7018 1913

#84
Living Room
Cuisines: Wine Bar, Lounge, Cafe
Average price: Modest
Area: Mayfair
Address: 3-9 Heddon Street
London W1B 4BE
Phone: 020 7292 0570

#85
Avenue
Cuisines: Wine Bar, British, European
Average price: Expensive
Area: St James's
Address: 7-9 St James's Street
London SW1A 1EE
Phone: 020 7321 2111

#86
The Bridge Wine Bar
Cuisines: Wine Bar
Average price: Modest
Area: Clapham
Address: 8 Voltaire Road
London SW4 6DH
Phone: 020 3632 6426

#87
Mug House
Cuisines: Wine Bar, British
Average price: Modest
Area: London Bridge
Address: 1-3 Tooley Street
London SE1 2PF
Phone: 020 7403 8343

#88
Camino
Cuisines: Tapas, Spanish, Wine Bar
Average price: Modest
Area: Southwark
Address: 5 Canvey Street
London SE1 9NA
Phone: 020 3617 3169

#89
Browns
Cuisines: Wine Bar, British
Average price: Modest
Area: Covent Garden, Strand
Address: 82-84 St Martins Lane
London WC2N 4AA
Phone: 020 7497 5050

#90
Fernandez & Wells
Cuisines: Coffee & Tea, Sandwiches
Average price: Inexpensive
Area: Soho
Address: 43 Lexington Street
London W1F 9AL
Phone: 020 7734 1546

#91
The 10 Cases
Cuisines: French
Average price: Expensive
Area: Covent Garden
Address: 16 Endell Street
London WC2H 9BD
Phone: 020 7836 6801

#92
Browns Bar & Brasserie
Cuisines: Wine Bar, British, Brasserie
Average price: Modest
Area: Westminster
Address: 2 Cardinal Walk
London SW1E 5AG
Phone: 020 7821 1450

#93
Quality Chop House
Cuisines: British, Wine Bar
Average price: Exclusive
Area: Clerkenwell
Address: 92-94 Farringdon Road
London EC1R 3EA
Phone: 020 7278 1452

#94
Vivat Bacchus
Cuisines: European, Wine Bar
Average price: Expensive
Area: London Bridge
Address: 4 Hays Lane
London SE1 2QE
Phone: 020 7234 0891

#95
El Vino Co
Cuisines: Wine Bar
Average price: Modest
Area: Blackfriars
Address: 30 New Bridge Street
London EC4V 6BJ
Phone: 020 7236 4534

#96
El Vino
Cuisines: Wine Bar
Average price: Modest
Area: Barbican
Address: 125 Bastion Highwalk
London EC2Y 5AP
Phone: 020 7600 6377

#97
Davys Gyngleboy
Cuisines: Wine Bar, British
Average price: Modest
Area: Paddington
Address: 27 Spring Street
London W2 1JA
Phone: 020 7723 3351

#98
Davy's Wine Vaults
Cuisines: Wine Bar, British
Average price: Expensive
Area: Greenwich
Address: 161-165 Greenwich High
Road, London SE10 8JA
Phone: 020 8858 7204

#99
Le Cochonnet
Cuisines: British, Italian, Wine Bar
Average price: Modest
Area: Maida Vale
Address: 1 Lauderdale Parade
London W9 1LU
Phone: 020 7289 0393

#100
Valentina
Cuisines: Italian, Wine Bar
Average price: Modest
Area: Wandsworth
Address: 75 Upper Richmond Road
London SW15 2SR
Phone: 020 8877 9906

#101
Enoteca Da Luca
Cuisines: Italian, Wine Bar
Average price: Inexpensive
Area: The City
Address: 10 - 12 Basinghall Street
London EC2V 5BQ
Phone: 020 7600 2161

#102
WC Wine & Charcuterie
Cuisines: Wine Bar
Average price: Modest
Area: Clapham Common
Address: Clapham Common
London SW4 7AA
Phone: 020 7622 5502

#103
Al Boccon Di'vino
Restaurant Wine Bar
Cuisines: Wine Bar
Average price: Expensive
Area: Richmond Upon Thames
Address: 14 Red Lion Street
London TW9 1RW
Phone: 020 8940 9060

#104
Willy's Wine Bar
Cuisines: Wine Bar, Cafe
Average price: Inexpensive
Area: Aldgate
Address: 107 Fenchurch Street
London EC3M 5JF
Phone: 020 7480 7289

#105
Monkeynuts
Cuisines: Steakhouse, Wine Bar
Average price: Modest
Area: Crouch End
Address: 2 Park Road
London N8 8TD
Phone: 020 8340 4466

#106
Toasted
Cuisines: Breakfast & Brunch, Wine
Bar, Beer, Wine & Spirits
Average price: Expensive
Area: East Dulwich
Address: 36-38 Lordship Lane
London SE22 8HJ
Phone: 020 8693 9021

#107
Fino's Wine Cellar
Cuisines: Wine Bar, Italian
Average price: Modest
Area: Mayfair
Address: 123 Mount Street
London W1K 3NP
Phone: 020 7491 1640

#108
Vale Victoria
Cuisines: Wine Bar, Tapas Bar,
Breakfast & Brunch
Average price: Modest
Area: Victoria
Address: 38 Buckingham Palace Road
London SW1W 0RE
Phone: 020 7834 1114

#109
All Bar One
Cuisines: Wine Bar
Average price: Modest
Area: Southwark, Waterloo
Address: 1 Chicheley Street
London SE1 7PY
Phone: 020 7921 9471

#110
Tartufi & Friends
Cuisines: Wine Bar, Italian
Average price: Exclusive
Area: Knightsbridge
Address: 87-135 Brompton Road
London SW1X 7XL
Phone: 020 7225 5800

#111
Mr Lawrence
Cuisines: Wine Bar
Average price: Modest
Area: Ladywell
Address: 389 Brockley Road
London SE4 2PH
Phone: 020 8692 1550

#112
Carvosso's At 210
Cuisines: British, Wine Bar
Average price: Expensive
Area: Chiswick
Address: 210 Chiswick High Road
London W4 1PD
Phone: 020 8995 9121

#113
Davy's
Cuisines: Wine Bar
Average price: Modest
Area: Canary Wharf, Isle of Dogs
Address: 31-35 Fishermans Walk
London E14 4DH
Phone: 020 7363 6633

#114
Bangers Bar and Grill
Cuisines: British, Wine Bar
Average price: Modest
Area: Liverpool Street / Broadgate
Address: 2-12 Wilson Street
London EC2M 2TE
Phone: 020 7377 6326

#115
Numidie Wine Bar and Bistro
Cuisines: Mediterranean, Wine Bar
Average price: Expensive
Area: Norwood (West & Upper)
Address: 48 Westow Hill
London SE19 1RX
Phone: 020 8766 6166

#116
Manouche Wine Bar
Cuisines: Wine Bar
Average price: Modest
Area: Fitzrovia
Address: 61 Goodge Street
London W1T 1TL
Phone: 020 7580 4005

#117
Ibérica
Cuisines: Spanish, Wine Bar
Average price: Expensive
Area: Farringdon
Address: 89 Turnmill Street
London EC1M 5QU
Phone: 020 7636 8650

#118
All Bar One
Cuisines: Wine Bar, Pub, British
Average price: Modest
Area: London Bridge, Shad Thames
Address: 34 Shad Thames
London SE1 2YG
Phone: 020 7940 9771

#119
Boyds Grill & Wine Bar
Cuisines: Wine Bar, Steakhouse
Average price: Modest
Area: Westminster
Address: 8 Northumberland Avenue
London WC2N 5BY
Phone: 020 7808 3344

#120
Olivocarne
Cuisines: Italian, Desserts, Wine Bar
Average price: Expensive
Area: Belgravia
Address: 61 Elizabeth Street
London SW1W 9PP
Phone: 020 7730 7997

#121
Tramontana Brindisa
Cuisines: Tapas Bar, Wine Bar
Average price: Modest
Area: Hoxton
Address: 152 Curtain Road
London EC2A 3AT
Phone: 020 7749 9961

#122
Crispins Wine Bar
Cuisines: Wine Bar
Average price: Modest
Area: Ealing
Address: 14 The Green
London W5 5DA
Phone: 020 8579 6912

#123
Theo's Pizzeria
Cuisines: Pizza, Wine Bar, Italian
Average price: Modest
Area: Camberwell
Address: 2 Grove Lane
London SE5 8SY
Phone: 020 3026 4224

#124
First Edition Wine Bar
Cuisines: Mediterranean, Wine Bar
Average price: Modest
Area: Canary Wharf, Isle of Dogs
Address: 25 Cabot Square
London E14 4QA
Phone: 020 7513 0300

#125
Star & Garter
Cuisines: Wine Bar
Average price: Modest
Area: Putney
Address: 4 Lower Richmond Road
London SW15 1JN
Phone: 020 8788 0345

#126
Edwin's Wine Bar
Cuisines: French, Wine Bar
Average price: Modest
Area: Liverpool Street / Broadgate
Address: 18 Phipp Street
London EC2A 4NU
Phone: 020 7739 4443

#127
The Popeseye
Cuisines: Wine Bar, Scottish,
Steakhouse
Average price: Expensive
Area: Archway
Address: 36 Highgate Hill
London N19 5NL
Phone: 020 3601 3830

#128
Balls Bros
Cuisines: Wine Bar
Average price: Modest
Area: Aldgate
Address: 158 Bishopsgate
London EC2M 4LX
Phone: 020 7426 0567

#129
Levante Bar
Cuisines: Wine Bar, Pub, Tapas Bar
Average price: Modest
Area: Canary Wharf, Isle of Dogs
Address: 14 Hertsmere Road
London E14 4AF
Phone: 020 3069 8981

#130
Julie's Restaurant and Bar
Cuisines: British, Wine Bar
Average price: Expensive
Area: Croydon
Address: 135 Portland Road
London W11 4LW
Phone: 020 7229 8331

#131
La Pizzica
Cuisines: Italian, Wine Bar
Average price: Modest
Area: Fulham
Address: 764-766 Fulham Road
London SW6 5HQ
Phone: 020 7731 3762

#132
Latymers
Cuisines: Wine Bar, Pub, Thai
Average price: Inexpensive
Area: West Kensington
Address: 157 Hammersmith Road
London W6 8BS
Phone: 020 8741 2507

#133
Polpo
Cuisines: Italian, Spanish, Wine Bar
Average price: Modest
Area: Farringdon
Address: 3 Cowcross Street
London EC1M 6DR
Phone: 020 7250 0034

#134
Ellory
Cuisines: Wine Bar, Bistros
Average price: Expensive
Area: London Fields
Address: 1 Westgate Street
London E8 3RL
Phone: 020 3095 9455

#135
Tiles
Cuisines: Wine Bar, European
Average price: Modest
Area: Westminster
Address: Buckingham Palace Rd 36
London SW1
Phone: 020 7834 7761

#136
Nottingdale
Cuisines: French, Wine Bar, Italian
Average price: Modest
Area: Shepherd's Bush
Address: 9 Nicholas Road
London W11 4AN
Phone: 020 7221 8020

#137
Daly's Wine Bar
Cuisines: Wine Bar, British
Average price: Modest
Area: Holborn
Address: 210 Strand
London WC2R 1AP
Phone: 020 7583 4476

#138
Wine Library
Cuisines: Wine Bar, Beer,
Wine & Spirits
Average price: Modest
Area: Aldgate, Tower Hill
Address: 43 Trinity Square
London EC3N 4DJ
Phone: 020 7481 0415

#139
Tom's Kitchen Terrace
Cuisines: Cocktail Bar, Wine Bar
Average price: Modest
Area: Strand
Address: Somerset House
London WC2R 0RN
Phone: 020 7845 4646

#140
Ibérica
Cuisines: Wine Bar, Spanish, Tapas
Average price: Expensive
Area: Fitzrovia
Address: 195 Great Portland Street
Marylebone W1W 5PS
Phone: 020 7636 8650

#141
The Olde Wine Shades
Cuisines: Wine Bar
Average price: Modest
Area: The City
Address: 6 Martin Lane
London EC4R 0DP
Phone: 020 7626 6876

#142
Pix
Cuisines: Tapas Bar, Lounge
Average price: Modest
Area: Covent Garden
Address: 63 Neal Street
London WC2H 9PJ
Phone: 020 7836 9779

#143
Mordens Wine Bar
Cuisines: Wine Bar
Average price: Modest
Area: Blackheath
Address: 7-9 Montpelier Vale
London SE3 0TA
Phone: 020 8852 0492

#144
All Bar One
Cuisines: Wine Bar
Average price: Modest
Area: Holborn
Address: 58 Kingsway
London WC2B 6DX
Phone: 020 7269 5171

#145
Davys City Boot
Cuisines: Wine Bar, British
Average price: Modest
Area: Barbican
Address: 7 Moorfields Highwalk
London EC2Y 9DP
Phone: 020 7588 4766

#146
All Bar One
Cuisines: Wine Bar
Average price: Modest
Area: Aldgate, Tower Hill
Address: 16 Byward Street
London EC3R 5BA
Phone: 020 7553 0301

#147
Corney & Barrow
Cuisines: Wine Bar
Average price: Modest
Area: Aldgate
Address: 25 Fenchurch Avenue
London EC3M 5BN
Phone: 020 7398 5870

#148
Bar 366 St John's Hill
Cuisines: Wine Bar
Average price: Modest
Area: Clapham Junction
Address: 126 St John's Hill
London SW11 1SL
Phone: 020 3538 2250

#149
Diciannove
Cuisines: Italian, Pizza, Wine Bar
Average price: Exclusive
Area: Blackfriars
Address: 19 New Bridge Street
London EC4V 6DB
Phone: 020 7438 8029

#150
All Bar One
Cuisines: Wine Bar
Average price: Modest
Area: Blackfriars
Address: 44-46 Ludgate Hill
London EC4M 7DE
Phone: 020 7653 9901

#151
Bar 191
Cuisines: Wine Bar
Average price: Modest
Area: Wimbledon
Address: 191 Worple Road
London SW20 8RE
Phone: 020 8944 5533

#152
York & Albany
Cuisines: Bar, British
Average price: Expensive
Area: Euston, Camden Town
Address: 127-129 Parkway
London NW1 7PS
Phone: 020 7592 1227

#153
Jamies Wine Bar
Cuisines: Wine Bar, Cafe
Average price: Modest
Area: Aldgate
Address: 18-22 Creechurch Lane
London EC3A 5AY
Phone: 020 7283 5836

#154
Revolution Leadenhall
Cuisines: Wine Bar, Dance Club
Average price: Expensive
Area: Aldgate
Address: Leadenhall Street
London EC3V 4QT
Phone: 020 7929 4233

#155
Orford Saloon Tapas Bar
Cuisines: Wine Bar, Spanish, Basque
Average price: Exclusive
Area: Walthamstow
Address: 32 Orford Road
London E17 9NJ
Phone: 020 8503 6542

#156
Davys At Canary Wharf
Cuisines: Wine Bar, British
Average price: Modest
Area: Bermondsey, Canada Water
Address: 31-35 Fishermans Walk
London E14 4DH
Phone: 020 7363 6633

#157
The Wine Theatre
Cuisines: Cafe, Wine Bar
Average price: Expensive
Area: Southwark
Address: 202-206 Union Street
London SE1 0LH
Phone: 020 7261 0209

#158
Greenwich Kitchen
Cuisines: Wine Bar
Average price: Modest
Area: Greenwich
Address: Peninsula Square
London SE10 0SQ
Phone: 020 8305 9757

#159
Corney & Barrow Bars
Cuisines: Wine Bar
Average price: Modest
Area: Aldgate
Address: 37 Jewry Street
London EC3N 2EX
Phone: 020 7680 8550

#160
The Nest
Cuisines: Wine Bar, Beer,
Wine & Spirits
Average price: Inexpensive
Area: Ealing
Address: 106-108 Uxbridge Road
London W7 3SU
Phone: 020 8579 7174

#161
Jamies
Cuisines: Wine Bar, British
Average price: Modest
Area: Barbican
Address: 25 Alban Gate
London EC2Y
Phone: 020 7600 0549

#162
Press House Wine Bars
Cuisines: Wine Bar, Cafe
Average price: Expensive
Area: Blackfriars, Holborn
Address: 1 ST. Brides Passage
London EC4Y 8EJ
Phone: 020 7353 5059

#163
**Davys Woolgate Bar
& Brasserie**
Cuisines: Wine Bar
Average price: Modest
Area: The City
Address: 25 Basinghall Street
London EC2V 5HA
Phone: 020 7600 5216

#164
203 Restaurant & Wine Bar
Cuisines: African, Wine Bar
Average price: Modest
Area: Streatham
Address: 203 Streatham High Road
London SW16 6EG
Phone: 020 8677 0003

#165
Corney & Barrow Bars
Cuisines: Wine Bar
Average price: Modest
Area: Aldgate
Address: 2b Eastcheap
London EC3M 1AB
Phone: 020 7929 3220

#166
Bow Wine Vaults
Cuisines: Wine Bar
Average price: Modest
Area: The City
Address: 10 Bow Church Yard
London EC4M 9DQ
Phone: 020 7248 1121

#167
Mas Q Menos
Cuisines: Wine Bar,
Tapas Bar, Spanish
Average price: Modest
Area: Aldgate
Address: 70 Mark Lane
London EC3R
Phone: 020 3778 0108

#168
Vindinista
Cuisines: Wine Bar
Average price: Modest
Area: Acton
Address: 74 Churchfield Road
London W3 6DH
Phone: 07703 502520

#169
Fanny Nelsons
Cuisines: Wine Bar, Pub
Average price: Modest
Area: Shoreditch, Bethnal Green
Address: 32 Horatio Street
London E2 7SB
Phone: 020 7613 4434

#170
The Gardens
Cuisines: Wine Bar
Average price: Modest
Area: West Hampstead
Address: 188 Broadhurst Gardens
London NW6 3AY
Phone: 020 7328 9833

#171
Balls Brothers
Cuisines: Wine Bar, Cafe, Pub
Average price: Modest
Area: Aldgate
Address: 2 St Mary At Hill
London EC3R 8EE
Phone: 020 7626 0321

#172
Bariba'
Cuisines: Wine Bar, Italian, Cafeteria
Average price: Inexpensive
Area: Battersea
Address: Battersea Park Road
London SW11 3BU
Phone: 07549 004375

#173
The New Zealand Cellar
Cuisines: Wine Bar, Beer,
Wine & Spirits
Average price: Modest
Area: Coldharbour Lane/ Herne Hill
Address: 49 Brixton Station Road
London SW9
Phone: 020 3633 3986

#174
Barrica
Cuisines: Tapas Bar, Spanish
Average price: Expensive
Area: Fitzrovia
Address: 62 Goodge Street
London W1T 4NE
Phone: 020 7436 9448

#175
Ciao Ciao
Cuisines: Wine Bar, Lounge
Average price: Modest
Area: West Hampstead
Address: 334 Kilburn High Road
London NW6 2QN
Phone: 020 3659 5210

#176
The Archduke Wine Bar
Cuisines: British, Bar
Average price: Expensive
Area: Southwark, Waterloo
Address: 153 Concert Hall Approach
London SE1 8XU
Phone: 020 7928 9370

#177
All Bar One
Cuisines: Wine Bar
Average price: Modest
Area: Covent Garden, Strand
Address: 19 Henrietta Street
London WC2E 8QH
Phone: 020 7240 9842

#178
Chinese Cricket Club
Cuisines: Chinese, Venue & Event
Space, Wine Bar
Average price: Modest
Area: Blackfriars, Holborn
Address: 19 New Bridge Street
London EC4V 6DB
Phone: 020 7438 8051

#179
Zenith Bar
Cuisines: Wine Bar
Average price: Modest
Area: Angel, Islington
Address: 125 Packington Street
London N1 7EA
Phone: 020 7226 1408

#180
Slug & Lettuce
Cuisines: Wine Bar, Pub
Average price: Modest
Area: Aldgate
Address: 100 Fenchurch Street
London EC3M 5JD
Phone: 020 7488 1890

#181
All Bar One
Cuisines: Wine Bar
Average price: Modest
Area: Covent Garden, Strand
Address: 19 Henrietta Street
London WC2E 8QH
Phone: 020 7557 7941

#182
Off The Cuff
Cuisines: Wine Bar, Music Venue
Average price: Modest
Area: Coldharbour Lane/ Herne Hill
Address: 301-303 Railton Road
London SE24 0JN
Phone: 07853 476235

#183
Waitrose Wine Bar
Cuisines: Wineries, Wine Bar
Average price: Modest
Area: Canary Wharf, Isle of Dogs
Address: 16-19 Canada Square
London E14 5EW
Phone: 020 7719 0300

#184
Fox & Grapes
Cuisines: Gastropub, Wine Bar
Average price: Exclusive
Area: Wimbledon Common
Address: 9 Camp Road
London SW19 4UN
Phone: 020 8619 1300

#185
Corney & Barrow Bars
Cuisines: Wine Bar
Average price: Expensive
Area: The City
Address: 12 Mason's Avenue
London EC2V 5BT
Phone: 020 7726 6030

#186
All Bar One
Cuisines: Wine Bar
Average price: Modest
Area: Liverpool Street / Broadgate
Address: 18-20 Appold Street
London EC2A 2AS
Phone: 020 7377 9671

#187
Davy's at White City
Cuisines: Wine Bar, Cafe
Average price: Expensive
Area: Shepherd's Bush, White City
Address: 201 Wood Lane
London W12 7TS
Phone: 020 8811 2862

#188
Donostia
Cuisines: Tapas
Average price: Expensive
Area: Marylebone
Address: 10 Seymour Place
London W1H 7ND
Phone: 020 3620 1845

#189
Tastour
Cuisines: Wine Bar, Social Club
Average price: Modest
Area: East Acton
Address: London W12 0TS
United Kingdom
Phone: 07919 053064

#190
All Bar One
Cuisines: Wine Bar
Average price: Modest
Area: Barbican, Liverpool Street
Address: 127 Finsbury Pavement
London EC2A 1NS
Phone: 020 7256 7577

#191
Hush
Cuisines: Bar, European
Average price: Expensive
Area: Mayfair
Address: 8 Lancashire Court
London W1S 1EY
Phone: 020 7659 1500

#192
Jamies
Cuisines: Wine Bar, Cafe
Average price: Expensive
Area: Aldgate, Tower Hill
Address: 119-121 Minories
London EC3N 1DR
Phone: 020 7709 9900

#193
Heeltap
Cuisines: Wine Bar
Average price: Modest
Area: Borough
Address: White Hart Yard
London SE1 1NX
Phone: 020 7407 2829

#194
Mama Jumbe's
Cuisines: African, Wine Bar
Average price: Modest
Area: East Ham
Address: 350 Katherine Road
London E7 8NW
Phone: 01277 800051

#195
Troyganic Cafe
Cuisines: Wine Bar, Cafe,
Music Venue
Average price: Modest
Area: Shoreditch
Address: 132 Kingsland Road
London E2 8DP
Phone: 07921 874443

#196
Jamies Wine Bar
Cuisines: Wine Bar
Average price: Modest
Area: Blackfriars
Address: 47 Ludgate Hill
London EC4M 7JZ
Phone: 020 7236 1942

#197
Corney & Barrow
Cuisines: Wine Bar
Average price: Modest
Area: Barbican
Address: 1 Ropemaker Street
London EC2Y 9HT
Phone: 020 7382 0606

#198
Roxie Steak and Wine Cafe
Cuisines: Steakhouse, Wine Bar
Average price: Modest
Area: Earlsfield
Address: 585 Garratt Lane
London SW18 4ST
Phone: 020 8944 9602

#199
Shepherd Market Wine House
Cuisines: Wine Bar
Average price: Modest
Area: Mayfair
Address: 21-23 Shepherd Market
West Central W1J 7PN
Phone: 020 7499 8555

#200
The Churchill Arms
Cuisines: Pub, Thai
Average price: Modest
Area: Notting Hill
Address: 119 Kensington Church
Street, London W8 7LN
Phone: 020 7727 4242

#201
The Abingdon
Cuisines: American
Average price: Expensive
Area: Kensington
Address: 54 Abingdon Road
London W8 6AP
Phone: 020 7937 3339

#202
All Bar One
Cuisines: Wine Bar
Average price: Expensive
Area: Marylebone
Address: 5-6 Picton Pl
London W1U 1BL
Phone: 020 7487 0161

#203
Admiral Codrington
Cuisines: Pub, British
Average price: Modest
Area: Chelsea
Address: 17 Mossop Street
London SW3 2LY
Phone: 020 7581 0005

#204
Corney & Barrow Bars
Cuisines: Wine Bar
Average price: Expensive
Area: Wapping
Address: 1 Thomas More Street
London E1W 1YZ
Phone: 020 7265 2400

#205
St John's Tavern
Cuisines: Gastropub, Pub
Average price: Expensive
Area: Tufnell Park, Upper Holloway
Address: 91 Junction Road
London N19 5QU
Phone: 020 7272 1587

#206
Camino
Cuisines: Bar, Spanish, Basque
Average price: Modest
Area: King's Cross
Address: 3 Varnishers Yard
London N1 9AF
Phone: 020 7841 7331

#207
Urban Tea Rooms
Cuisines: British, Bar, Coffee & Tea
Average price: Modest
Area: Soho
Address: 19 Kingly Street
London W1B 5PY
Phone: 020 7434 3767

#208
All Bar One
Cuisines: Wine Bar
Average price: Modest
Area: The City
Address: 103 Cannon Street
London EC4N 5AD
Phone: 020 7220 9031

#209
The Slug and Lettuce - O2
Cuisines: Fish & Chips, Wine Bar,
Cocktail Bar
Average price: Expensive
Area: Greenwich
Address: 1-34 Entertainment Ave
London SE10 0DY
Phone: 0845 126 2990

#210
Bar Capitale 2
Cuisines: Wine Bar, Pizza, Italian
Average price: Modest
Area: The City
Address: 1 Poultry
London EC2R 8EJ
Phone: 020 7248 3117

#211
Opera Tavern
Cuisines: Tapas Bar
Average price: Expensive
Area: Covent Garden, Strand
Address: 23 Catherine Street
London WC2B 5JS
Phone: 020 7836 3680

#212
Cinnamon Culture
Cuisines: Indian, Food, Wine Bar
Average price: Modest
Area: Sundridge
Address: 46 Plaistow Lane
London BR1 3PA
Phone: 020 8289 0322

#213
Texture
Cuisines: Champagne Bar,
European, Gastropub
Average price: Expensive
Area: Marylebone
Address: 34 Portman Street
London W1H 7BY
Phone: 020 7224 0028

#214
Corney & Barrow Bars
Cuisines: Wine Bar
Average price: Modest
Area: Blackfriars
Address: 10 Paternoster Square
London EC4M 7DX
Phone: 020 7618 9520

#215
José
Cuisines: Spanish, Tapas Bar
Average price: Modest
Area: Borough
Address: 104 Bermondsey Street
London SE1 3UB
Phone: 020 7403 4902

#216
The Dairy
Cuisines: Bar, British
Average price: Exclusive
Area: Clapham
Address: 15 The Pavement
London SW4 0HY
Phone: 020 7622 4165

#217
All Bar One
Cuisines: Wine Bar
Average price: Modest
Area: Westminster
Address: 28-30 London Bridge Street
London SE1 9SG
Phone: 020 403 8494

#218
Marquis Of Westminster
Cuisines: British, Pub, Cocktail Bar
Average price: Modest
Area: Pimlico
Address: 50 Warwick Way
London SW1V 1RY
Phone: 020 7828 1700

#219
All Bar One
Cuisines: Wine Bar
Average price: Modest
Area: Marylebone
Address: 7-9 Paddington Street
London W1U 5QH
Phone: 020 7487 0071

#220
Leonardo Wine Bar
Cuisines: Wine Bar, British
Average price: Modest
Area: Roehampton
Address: 459 Upper Richmond Road
W, London SW14 7PS
Phone: 020 8878 3480

#221
Icebar London
Cuisines: European, Lounge
Average price: Modest
Area: Mayfair
Address: 31-33 Heddon Street
London W1B 4BN
Phone: 020 7478 8910

#222
Bilbao Berria
Cuisines: Spanish, Basque, Tapas Bar
Average price: Modest
Area: St James's
Address: 2 Lower Regent St
London SW1Y 4LR
Phone: 020 7930 8408

#223
The Bird In Hand
Cuisines: Pub, Italian
Average price: Modest
Area: West Kensington
Address: 88 Masbro Road
London W14 0LR
Phone: 020 7371 2721

#224
Holborn Grind
Cuisines: Cocktail Bar, Coffee & Tea,
Breakfast & Brunch
Average price: Modest
Area: Covent Garden
Address: 199 High Holborn
London WC1V 7BD
Phone: 020 3693 3400

#225
The Princess Of Wales
Cuisines: Pub, British
Average price: Modest
Area: Strand
Address: 27 Villiers Street
London WC2N 6ND
Phone: 020 7484 0748

#226
The Drunken Monkey
Cuisines: Dim Sum, Lounge,
Cocktail Bar
Average price: Modest
Area: Liverpool Street / Broadgate
Address: 222 Shoreditch High Street
London E1 6PJ
Phone: 020 7392 9606

#227
The Square Pig
Cuisines: Pub, British
Average price: Inexpensive
Area: Bloomsbury
Address: 30-32 Procter Street
London WC1V 6NX
Phone: 020 7691 3144

#228
Hix - Soho
Cuisines: British, Bar
Average price: Expensive
Area: Soho
Address: 66-70 Brewer Street
London W1F 9UP
Phone: 020 7292 3518

#229
The Cinnamon Club
Cuisines: Indian, Cocktail Bar
Average price: Exclusive
Area: Westminster
Address: 30-32 Great Smith Street
London SW1P 3BU
Phone: 020 7222 2555

#230
Firefly Bar & Thai kitchen
Cuisines: Bar, Thai
Average price: Modest
Area: Balham
Address: 3 Station Parade
London SW12 9AZ
Phone: 020 8673 9796

#231
G & Tea
Cuisines: Cocktail Bar, Lounge, Wine Bar
Average price: Modest
Area: Canary Wharf, Isle of Dogs, Poplar
Address: 22 Hertsmere Road London E14 4ED
Phone: 020 7517 2858

#232
Portobello Gold
Cuisines: Pub, Guest Houses, British
Average price: Modest
Area: Notting Hill
Address: 95-97 Portobello Road London W11 2QB
Phone: 020 7460 4900

#233
Androuet
Cuisines: Cheese Shop, Bar
Average price: Modest
Area: Spitalfields
Address: 10A Lamb Street London E1 6EA
Phone: 020 7247 7437

#234
Roast
Cuisines: British, Bar
Average price: Expensive
Area: London Bridge
Address: Stoney Street London SE1 1TL
Phone: 020 3006 6111

#235
Brasserie Zédel
Cuisines: Brasserie, Jazz & Blues, Cocktail Bar
Average price: Modest
Area: Soho
Address: 20 Sherwood Street London W1F 7ED
Phone: 020 7734 4888

#236
Princess Victoria
Cuisines: Gastropub, Venue & Event Space, Pub
Average price: Modest
Area: Acton
Address: 217 Uxbridge Road London W12 9DH
Phone: 020 8749 5886

#237
The Gorgeous Kitchen
Cuisines: British, Breakfast & Brunch, Wine Bar
Average price: Expensive
Area: Heathrow
Address: Heathrow Airport London TW6 1EW
Phone: 07795 636840

#238
Scooter Caffè
Cuisines: Bar, Cafe
Average price: Inexpensive
Area: Southwark, Waterloo
Address: 132 Lower Marsh London SE1 7AE
Phone: 020 7620 1421

#239
All Bar One
Cuisines: Wine Bar
Average price: Modest
Area: Fitzrovia, Marylebone
Address: 289-293 Regent Street London W1B 2HJ
Phone: 020 7636 8197

#240
Safari
Cuisines: Wine Bar, African
Average price: Modest
Area: Streatham
Address: 440 Streatham High Road London SW16 3PX
Phone: 020 8679 9055

#241
Benugo @ BFI
Cuisines: Bar, British
Average price: Modest
Area: South Bank, Southwark
Address: 2166 Belvedere Rd
London SE1 8XT
Phone: 020 7928 3232

#242
Condesa
Cuisines: Tapas, Spanish
Average price: Modest
Area: Covent Garden, Strand
Address: 15 Maiden Lane
London WC2E 7NG
Phone: 020 3601 5752

#243
The Junction Tavern
Cuisines: Pub, Gastropub
Average price: Modest
Area: Kentish Town
Address: 101 Fortess Road
London NW5 1AG
Phone: 020 7485 9400

#244
Rabot 1745
Cuisines: Coffee & Tea, American
Average price: Modest
Area: London Bridge
Address: 2-4 Bedale Street
London SE1 9AL
Phone: 020 7378 8226

#245
Meat Liquor
Cuisines: Burgers, American
Average price: Modest
Area: Marylebone
Address: 74 Welbeck Street
London W1G 0BA
Phone: 020 7224 4239

#246
45 Jermyn St
Cuisines: British, Bar
Average price: Expensive
Area: St James's
Address: 45 Jermyn Street
London SW1Y 6JD
Phone: 020 7205 4545

#247
Chi Noodle
Cuisines: Chinese, Bar
Average price: Modest
Area: Blackfriars, Holborn
Address: 5 New Bridge Street
London EC4V 6AB
Phone: 020 7353 2409

#248
Roxy Bar & Screen
Cuisines: Bar, Cinema, British
Average price: Modest
Area: Borough
Address: 128-132 Borough High Street
London SE1 1LB
Phone: 020 7407 4057

#249
The Prince of Wales
Cuisines: Pub, British
Average price: Modest
Area: Wimbledon
Address: 2 Hartfield Rd
London SW19 3TA
Phone: 020 8946 5369

#250
Grand Union Camden
Cuisines: Burgers, Pizza, Cocktail Bar
Average price: Modest
Area: Camden Town
Address: 102-104 Camden Road
London NW1 9EA
Phone: 020 7485 4530

#251
La Farola
Cuisines: Tapas, Spanish
Average price: Modest
Area: Angel, Islington
Address: 101 Upper Street
London N1 1QN
Phone: 020 7359 7707

#252
Pond Dalston
Cuisines: Hawaiian, Bar, Pop-Up Cafe
Average price: Expensive
Area: De Beauvoir, Kingsland
Address: 3 Gillett Street
London N16 8JH
Phone: 020 3772 6727

#253
Nicholas Wine Bar
Cuisines: Wine Bar
Average price: Inexpensive
Area: Canary Wharf, Isle of Dogs
Address: 1 Canada Square
London E14 5AX
Phone: 020 7512 9283

#254
Sketch
Cuisines: French, Cocktail Bar
Average price: Expensive
Area: Mayfair
Address: 9 Conduit Street
London W1S 2XG
Phone: 020 7659 4500

#255
Searcy's St Pancras Grand
Restaurant and Champagne Bar
Cuisines: Champagne Bar, Brasserie
Average price: Expensive
Area: King's Cross
Address: Grand Terrace Upper
Concourse
London N1C 4QL
Phone: 020 7870 9900

#256
All Bar One
Cuisines: Wine Bar
Average price: Modest
Area: Richmond Upon Thames
Address: 11-13 Hill Street
Richmond TW9 1SX
Phone: 020 8332 7141

#257
The Albion
Cuisines: Pub, Gastropub
Average price: Expensive
Area: Islington
Address: 10 Thornhill Road
London N1 1HW
Phone: 020 7607 7450

#258
Boisdale of Belgravia
Cuisines: British, Lounge,
Jazz & Blues
Average price: Expensive
Area: Belgravia
Address: 15 Eccleston Street
London SW1W 9LX
Phone: 020 7730 6922

#259
Henry's Cafe Bar
Cuisines: Lounge, Cafe
Average price: Modest
Area: Covent Garden, Strand
Address: 5/6 Henrietta Street
London WC2E 8PS
Phone: 07557 740183

#260
The Orchard
Cuisines: Bar, British
Average price: Modest
Area: Lewisham
Address: 5 Harefield Road
London SE4 1LW
Phone: 020 8692 4756

#261
Bubbledogs
Cuisines: Hot Dogs, Champagne Bar
Average price: Modest
Area: Fitzrovia
Address: 70 Charlotte Street
London W1T 4QG
Phone: 020 7637 7770

#262
Tanner and Co
Cuisines: Bar, British
Average price: Modest
Area: Borough
Address: 50 Bermondsey Street
London SE1 3UD
Phone: 020 7357 0244

#263
Old Bengal Bar
Cuisines: British, Bar
Average price: Expensive
Area: Aldgate
Address: 16A New Street
London EC2M 4TR
Phone: 020 3503 0780

#264
Coya
Cuisines: Peruvian,
Latin American, Lounge
Average price: Exclusive
Area: Mayfair
Address: 118 Piccadilly
London W1J 7NW
Phone: 020 7042 7118

#265
Patch
Cuisines: Seafood, Cocktail Bar
Average price: Modest
Area: Blackfriars
Address: 58-60 Carter Lane
London EC4V 5EA
Phone: 020 7489 7777

#266
Pix
Cuisines: Spanish, Bar
Average price: Modest
Area: Soho
Address: 16 Bateman Street
London W1D 3AH
Phone: 020 7437 0377

#267
Piäno
Cuisines: Cocktail Bar,
Piano Bar, American
Average price: Expensive
Area: Kensington
Address: 106 Kensington High Street
London W8 4SG
Phone: 020 7938 4664

#268
Satay Cocktail Bar & Restaurant
Cuisines: Indonesian, Bar, Malaysian
Average price: Modest
Area: Brixton, Coldharbour Lane
Address: 447 Coldharbour Lane
London SW9 8LP
Phone: 0844 474 6080

#269
Hoxton Grill
Cuisines: Lounge, American
Average price: Modest
Area: Liverpool Street / Broadgate
Address: 81 Great Eastern Street
London EC2A 3HU
Phone: 020 7739 9111

#270
Bavarian Beerhouse
Cuisines: Bar, British
Average price: Modest
Area: Islington
Address: 190 City Road
London EC1V 2QH
Phone: 0844 330 2005

#271
The Clove Club
Cuisines: British, Cocktail Bar
Average price: Exclusive
Area: Hoxton
Address: Shoreditch Town Hall
London EC1V 9LT
Phone: 020 7729 6496

#272
Dabbous
Cuisines: European, Bar
Average price: Exclusive
Area: Fitzrovia
Address: 39 Whitfield Street
London W1T 2SF
Phone: 020 7323 1544

#273
Tollington The Public House
Cuisines: Pub, Gastropub, Thai
Average price: Modest
Area: Lower Holloway
Address: 115 Hornsey Road
London N7 6DN
Phone: 020 7700 6419

#274
All Bar One
Cuisines: Cafe, Nightlife
Average price: Modest
Area: Strand
Address: 6 Villiers Street
London WC2N 6NQ
Phone: 020 7839 9239

#275
The Jam Tree
Cuisines: British, Gastropub,
Cocktail Bar
Average price: Modest
Area: West Brompton
Address: 541 Kings Road
London SW6 2EB
Phone: 020 3397 3739

#276
Woody's Bar & Kitchen
Cuisines: Wine Bar
Average price: Modest
Area: Kingston Upon Thames
Address: 5 Ram Passage
Kingston upon Thames KT1 1HH
Phone: 020 8541 4984

#277
The Bridge
Cuisines: Coffee & Tea,
Sandwiches, Lounge
Average price: Modest
Area: Hoxton
Address: 15 Kingsland Road
London E2 8AA
Phone: 0871 963 4200

#278
Rules Restaurant
Cuisines: British, Bar
Average price: Expensive
Area: Covent Garden, Strand
Address: 35 Maiden Lane
London WC2E 7LB
Phone: 020 7836 5314

#279
Boro Bistro
Cuisines: Pub, French
Average price: Modest
Area: London Bridge
Address: 6-10 Borough High Street
London SE1 9QQ
Phone: 020 7378 0788

#280
The Cuban
Cuisines: Bar, Cuban
Average price: Modest
Area: Camden Town, Chalk Farm
Address: Chalk Farm Road
London NW1 8AH
Phone: 033 3240 2000

#281
Morito
Cuisines: Tapas, Spanish
Average price: Modest
Area: Clerkenwell
Address: 32 Exmouth Market
London EC1R 4QE
Phone: 020 7278 7007

#282
Antico Restaurant
Cuisines: Italian, Bar
Average price: Modest
Area: Borough
Address: 214 Bermondsey Street
London SE1 3TQ
Phone: 020 7407 4682

#283
Bob Bob Ricard
Cuisines: British, Russian, Bar
Average price: Expensive
Area: Soho
Address: 1 Upper St James Street
London W1F 9DF
Phone: 020 3145 1000

#284
Puncheon
Cuisines: Pub, British
Average price: Modest
Area: Farringdon
Address: Unit 5 Cowcross Pl
London EC1M 6DQ
Phone: 020 7250 3336

#285
Apero Restaurant and Bar
Cuisines: Mediterranean,
Breakfast & Brunch, Bar
Average price: Modest
Area: South Kensington
Address: 2 Harrington Road
London SW7 3ER
Phone: 020 7591 4410

#286
Oblix At The Shard
Cuisines: Lounge, European
Average price: Exclusive
Area: London Bridge
Address: 31 St Thomas Street
London SE1 9SY
Phone: 020 7268 6700

#287
Graveney & Meadow
Cuisines: Cocktail Bar, Gastropub,
Breakfast & Brunch
Average price: Inexpensive
Area: Tooting, Tooting Broadway
Address: 40 Mitcham Road
London SW17 9NA
Phone: 020 8672 9016

#288
Momo
Cuisines: Moroccan, Bar,
Breakfast & Brunch
Average price: Expensive
Area: Mayfair
Address: 25-27 Heddon Street
London W1B 4BH
Phone: 020 7434 4040

#289
Amuse Bouche
Cuisines: Champagne Bar, British
Average price: Modest
Area: Fulham
Address: 51 Parsons Green Lane
London SW6 4JA
Phone: 020 7371 8517

#290
Gymkhana
Cuisines: Indian, Cocktail Bar
Average price: Exclusive
Area: Mayfair
Address: 42 Albemarle Street
London W1S 4JH
Phone: 020 3011 5900

#291
Browns
Cuisines: Cafe
Average price: Modest
Area: The City
Address: 8 Old Jewry
London EC2R 8DN
Phone: 020 7606 6677

#292
The Fat Bear
Cuisines: American, Soul Food,
Barbeque
Average price: Modest
Area: Blackfriars
Address: 61 Carter Lane
London EC4V 5DY
Phone: 020 7236 2498

#293
Blacklock
Cuisines: British, Cocktail Bar,
Steakhouse
Average price: Exclusive
Area: Soho
Address: 24 Great Windmill Street
London W1D 7LG
Phone: 020 3441 6996

#294
Polpo
Cuisines: Italian, Bar
Average price: Modest
Area: Soho
Address: 41 Beak Street
London W1F 9SB
Phone: 020 7734 4479

#295
Most Café Bar
Cuisines: British, Cocktail Bar
Average price: Modest
Area: London Bridge, Shad Thames
Address: 206-208 Tower Bridge Road
London SE1 2UP
Phone: 020 7403 6030

#296
The Saint
Cuisines: British, Bar
Average price: Modest
Area: Blackfriars
Address: Rose Street
London EC4M 7DQ
Phone: 020 7600 5500

#297
The Shakespeare
Cuisines: Pub, Italian, Pizza
Average price: Modest
Area: Barbican
Address: 2 Goswell Road
London EC1M 7AA
Phone: 020 7253 6116

#298
Duck & Waffle
Cuisines: European, Bar
Average price: Expensive
Area: Liverpool Street / Broadgate
Address: 110 Bishopsgate
London EC2N 4AY
Phone: 020 3640 7310

#299
Fire Station
Cuisines: Pub, European
Average price: Modest
Area: Southwark, Waterloo
Address: 150 Waterloo Road
London SE1 8SB
Phone: 020 7620 2226

#300
Simpson's In The Strand
Cuisines: British, Bar
Average price: Expensive
Area: Strand
Address: 100 Strand
London WC2R 0EW
Phone: 020 7836 9112

#301
Hawksmoor Guildhall
Cuisines: Steakhouse, Bar, British
Average price: Expensive
Area: The City
Address: 10 Basinghall Street
London EC2V 5BQ
Phone: 020 7397 8120

#302
Garlic & Shots
Cuisines: Bar, Scandinavian
Average price: Modest
Area: Soho
Address: 14 Frith Street
London W1D 4RD
Phone: 020 7734 9505

#303
Hélène Darroze
Cuisines: Bar, French
Average price: Exclusive
Area: Mayfair
Address: 16 Carlos Place
London W1K 2AL
Phone: 020 3147 7200

#304
Bar Pepito
Cuisines: Bar
Average price: Modest
Area: King's Cross
Address: 3 Varnishers Yard
London N1 9FD
Phone: 020 7841 7331

#305
Lobos Meat and Tapas
Cuisines: Tapas, Tapas Bar, Spanish
Average price: Expensive
Area: London Bridge
Address: 14 Borough High Street
London SE1 9QG
Phone: 020 7407 5361

#306
Earlham Street Clubhouse
Cuisines: Pizza, Cocktail Bar
Average price: Modest
Area: Covent Garden
Address: 35 Earlham Street
London WC2H 9LS
Phone: 020 7240 5142

#307
Christopher's
Cuisines: American, Bar, British
Average price: Modest
Area: Covent Garden, Strand
Address: 18 Wellington Street
London WC2E 7DD
Phone: 020 7240 4222

#308
The Social
Cuisines: Bar, Dance Club,
Music Venue
Average price: Modest
Area: Fitzrovia
Address: 5 Little Portland Street
London W1W 7JD
Phone: 020 7636 4992

#309
Melanzana
Cuisines: Italian, Bar, Delis
Average price: Modest
Area: Battersea
Address: 140 Westbridge Road
London SW11 3PF
Phone: 020 7228 5420

#310
Mint Leaf
Cuisines: Indian, Pakistani, Bar
Average price: Expensive
Area: Trafalgar Square
Address: 4 Suffolk Place
London SW1Y 4HX
Phone: 020 7930 9020

#311
Salvador & Amanda
Cuisines: Spanish, Bar
Average price: Modest
Area: Covent Garden
Address: 8 Great Newport Street
London WC2H 7JA
Phone: 020 7240 1551

#312
Soho Grind
Cuisines: Coffee & Tea, Cafe,
Cocktail Bar
Average price: Inexpensive
Area: Soho
Address: 19 Beak Street
London W1F 9RP
Phone: 020 7287 7073

#313
The Riding House Café
Cuisines: British, Bar
Average price: Modest
Area: Fitzrovia
Address: 43-51 Great Tichfield Street
London W1W 7PQ
Phone: 020 7927 0840

#314
Big Easy
Cuisines: American, Bar, Music Venue
Average price: Modest
Area: Chelsea
Address: 332-334 Kings Road
London SW3 5UR
Phone: 020 7352 4071

#315
Refuel Bar & Restaurant
Cuisines: Bar, European
Average price: Expensive
Area: Soho
Address: 4 Richmond Mews
London W1D 3DH
Phone: 020 7559 3007

#316
The Lost Angel
Cuisines: Bar, Steakhouse
Average price: Modest
Area: Battersea
Address: 339 Battersea Park Road
London SW11 4LS
Phone: 020 7622 2112

#317
Kettner's
Cuisines: European, Champagne Bar
Average price: Expensive
Area: Bloomsbury
Address: 29 Romilly Street
London W1D 5HP
Phone: 020 7734 6112

#318
Powder Keg Diplomacy
Cuisines: Bar, British
Average price: Expensive
Area: Clapham Junction
Address: 147 St John's Hill
London SW11 1TQ
Phone: 020 7450 6457

#319
SW9
Cuisines: Bar, Mediterranean, Cafe
Average price: Modest
Area: Stockwell
Address: 11 Dorrell Place
London SW9 8EG
Phone: 020 7738 3116

#320
Brilliant Corners
Cuisines: Bar, Japanese, Sushi Bar
Average price: Modest
Area: Dalston
Address: 470 Kingsland Road
London E8 4AE
Phone: 020 7812 9511

#321
Lucky Voice Karaoke
Cuisines: Karaoke, Bar, Pizza
Average price: Modest
Area: Islington
Address: 173-174 Upper Street
London N1 1RG
Phone: 020 7354 6280

#322
The Cut
Cuisines: Bar, Coffee & Tea,
Breakfast & Brunch
Average price: Modest
Area: Southwark, Waterloo
Address: 66 The Cut
London SE1 8LZ
Phone: 020 7928 4400

#323
Bar Termini
Cuisines: Bar
Average price: Modest
Area: Bloomsbury
Address: 7 Old Compton Street
London W1D 5JE
Phone: 07860 945018

#324
The Gallery
Cuisines: British, Bar
Average price: Modest
Area: West Hampstead
Address: 190 Broadhurst Gardens
London NW6 3AY
Phone: 020 7625 9184

#325
Mestizo
Cuisines: Mexican, Bar
Average price: Modest
Area: Euston
Address: 103 Hampstead Road
London NW1 3EL
Phone: 020 7387 4064

#326
Quo Vadis
Cuisines: British, Cocktail Bar
Average price: Expensive
Area: Soho
Address: 26-29 Dean Street
London W1D 3LL
Phone: 020 7437 9585

#327
Meat People
Cuisines: Steakhouse, Bar, Seafood
Average price: Modest
Area: Angel, Islington
Address: 4-6 Essex Road
London N1 8LN
Phone: 020 7359 5361

#328
The Bull & Last
Cuisines: Bar, Gastropub
Average price: Expensive
Area: Parliament Hill/Dartmouth Park
Address: 168 Highgate Road
London NW5 1QS
Phone: 020 7267 3641

#329
CUT at 45 Park Lane
Cuisines: American, Steakhouse, Bar
Average price: Exclusive
Area: Mayfair
Address: 45 Park Lane
London W1K 1PN
Phone: 020 7493 4554

#330
108 Bar & Grill
Cuisines: British, European,
Cocktail Bar
Average price: Expensive
Area: Marylebone
Address: 108 Marylebone Lane
London W1U 2QE
Phone: 020 7969 3900

#331
Cinnamon Kitchen
Cuisines: Indian, Cocktail Bar
Average price: Expensive
Area: Aldgate
Address: 9 Devonshire Square
London EC2M 4YL
Phone: 020 7626 5000

#332
Bibendum
Cuisines: Bar, Seafood, European
Average price: Expensive
Area: Chelsea
Address: 81 Fulham Road
London SW3 6RD
Phone: 020 7589 1480

#333
Akari
Cuisines: Japanese, Bar
Average price: Modest
Area: Canonbury
Address: 196 Essex Road
London N1 8LZ
Phone: 020 7226 9943

#334
Big Easy
Cuisines: Barbeque, Seafood,
American
Average price: Modest
Area: Covent Garden, Strand
Address: 12 Maiden Lane
London WC2E 7NA
Phone: 020 3728 4888

#335
606 Club
Cuisines: Jazz & Blues,
Music Venue, American
Average price: Modest
Area: West Brompton
Address: 90 Lots Road
London SW10 0QD
Phone: 020 7352 5953

#336
Hazelnut Fleurs
Cuisines: Wine Bar
Average price: Modest
Area: Eden Park
Address: 124 Croydon Road
Beckenham BR3 4DF
Phone: 020 8663 3385

#337
Flesh & Buns
Cuisines: Japanese, Bar
Average price: Expensive
Area: Covent Garden
Address: 41 Earlham Street
London WC2H 9LX
Phone: 020 7632 9500

#338
Plateau Restaurant
Cuisines: Bar, British, French,
European, Burgers
Average price: Expensive
Area: Canary Wharf, Isle of Dogs
Address: Canada Place
London E14 5ER
Phone: 020 7715 7100

#339
**Booking Office Bar
& Restaurant**
Cuisines: Bar, European, British
Average price: Expensive
Area: King's Cross
Address: Euston Road
London NW1 2AR
Phone: 020 7841 3540

#340
Crocker's Folly
Cuisines: Gastropub, Bar
Average price: Expensive
Area: Lisson Grove
Address: 24 Aberdeen Place
London NW8 8JR
Phone: 020 7289 9898

#341
Electric Diner
Cuisines: American, Cocktail Bar
Average price: Modest
Area: Notting Hill
Address: 191 Portobello Road
London W11 2ED
Phone: 020 7908 9696

#342
Zuma
Cuisines: Japanese, Lounge
Average price: Exclusive
Area: Knightsbridge
Address: 5 Raphael Street
London SW7 1DL
Phone: 020 7584 1010

#343
Holborn Dining Room
Cuisines: British, Delis, Bar
Average price: Expensive
Area: Holborn
Address: 252 High Holborn
London WC1V 7EN
Phone: 020 3747 8633

#344
Madison
Cuisines: European, Lounge
Average price: Expensive
Area: The City
Address: 1 New Change
London EC4M 9AF
Phone: 020 8305 3088

#345
Gillray's Steakhouse & Bar
Cuisines: Bar, Steakhouse
Average price: Expensive
Area: South Bank, Southwark
Address: Westminster Bridge Road
London SE1 7PB
Phone: 020 7902 8000

#346
The Waterside
Cuisines: Pub, Gastropub
Average price: Modest
Area: Fulham
Address: The Boulevard
London SW6 2SU
Phone: 020 7371 0802

#347
Asia de Cuba Restaurant
Cuisines: Asian Fusion, Cuban, Bar
Average price: Expensive
Area: Covent Garden, Strand
Address: 45 St Martin's Lane
London WC2N 4HX
Phone: 020 7300 5500

#348
The Blues Kitchen
Cuisines: American, Bar, Music Venue
Average price: Modest
Area: Hoxton
Address: 134-146 Curtain Road
London EC2A 3AR
Phone: 020 7729 7216

#349
Isarn
Cuisines: Thai, Bar
Average price: Modest
Area: Angel, Islington
Address: 119 Upper Street
London N1 1QP
Phone: 020 7424 5153

#350
Rucoletta
Cuisines: Bar, Italian
Average price: Modest
Area: The City
Address: 6 Foster Lane
London EC2V 6HH
Phone: 020 7600 7776

#351
The Warrington Hotel
Cuisines: Specialty Food, Pub, Cafe
Average price: Expensive
Area: Maida Vale
Address: 93 Warrington Crescent
London SW8 3JD
Phone: 020 7592 7960

#352
Beagle
Cuisines: Bar, British, Coffee & Tea
Average price: Modest
Area: Haggerston
Address: 397 - 399 Geffrye Street
London E2 8HZ
Phone: 020 7613 2967

#353
Seven at Brixton
Cuisines: Spanish, Lounge,
Cocktail Bar
Average price: Modest
Area: Coldharbour Lane/ Herne Hill
Address: Unit 7
London SW9 8LB
Phone: 020 7998 3309

#354
The Alchemist
Cuisines: Cocktail Bar, British
Average price: Modest
Area: Aldgate
Address: 6 Bevis Marks
London EC3A 7HL
Phone: 020 7283 8800

#355
Salt Bar
Cuisines: Cafe, Bar
Average price: Expensive
Area: Paddington
Address: 13 Edgware Road
London W2 2JE
Phone: 020 7402 1155

#356
Sky Pod Bar
Cuisines: British, Cocktail Bar
Average price: Modest
Area: Aldgate
Address: Floor 35 20 Fenchurch Street
London EC3M 3BY
Phone: 033 3772 0020

#357
Sartoria
Cuisines: Italian, Bar
Average price: Exclusive
Area: Mayfair
Address: 20 Savile Row
London W1S 3PR
Phone: 020 7534 7000

#358
Clockjack
Cuisines: Chicken Wings,
European, American
Average price: Modest
Area: Soho
Address: 14 Denman Street
London W1D 7HJ
Phone: 020 7287 5111

#359
Jackson + Rye
Cuisines: American, Steakhouse,
Cocktail Bar
Average price: Modest
Area: Soho
Address: 56 Wardour Street
London W1D 4JG
Phone: 020 7437 8338

#360
Cheyne Walk Brasserie
Cuisines: French, Bar
Average price: Exclusive
Area: Chelsea
Address: 50 Cheyne Walk
London SW3 5LR
Phone: 020 7376 8787

#361
Crate Brewery
Cuisines: Pizza, Breweries, Bar
Average price: Modest
Area: Stratford
Address: Unit 7 Queens Yard Hackney
London E9 5EN
Phone: 07834 275687

#362
Charlotte Street Hotel
Cuisines: Hotels, European, Lounge
Average price: Expensive
Area: Fitzrovia
Address: 15-17 Charlotte Street
London W1T 1RJ
Phone: 020 7806 2000

#363
The Anthologist
Cuisines: American, British, Burgers
Average price: Modest
Area: The City
Address: 58 Gresham Street
London EC2V 7BB
Phone: 0845 468 0101

#364
Hubbard & Bell
Cuisines: Bar, British, Cafe
Average price: Modest
Area: Covent Garden
Address: 199-206 High Holborn
London WC1V 7BD
Phone: 020 7661 3030

#365
Sophie's Steakhouse & Bar
Cuisines: Steakhouse, American
Average price: Modest
Area: Chelsea
Address: 311-313 Fulham Road
London SW10 9QH
Phone: 020 7352 0088

#366
Bounce Farringdon
Cuisines: Pizza, Bar
Average price: Modest
Area: Farringdon
Address: 121 Holborn
London EC1N 2TD
Phone: 020 3657 6525

#367
All Bar One
Cuisines: Wine Bar
Average price: Modest
Area: Sutton
Address: 2 Hill Road
Sutton SM1 1DZ
Phone: 020 8652 3521

#368
Buddha-Bar London
Cuisines: Asian Fusion, Venue &
Event Space, Cocktail Bar
Average price: Exclusive
Area: Hyde Park, Knightsbridge
Address: 145 Knightsbridge
London SW1X 7PA
Phone: 020 3667 5222

#369
Translate
Cuisines: Cafe, Cocktail Bar
Average price: Modest
Area: Shoreditch
Address: 12-14 Kingsland Road
London E2 8DA
Phone: 020 3487 0796

#370
Frederick's
Cuisines: French, British, Cocktail Bar
Average price: Expensive
Area: Angel, Islington
Address: 106 Islington High Street
London N1 8EG
Phone: 020 7359 2888

#371
Hotel Café Royal
Cuisines: Hotels, Cafe, Bar
Average price: Expensive
Area: Soho
Address: 68 Regent Street
London W1B 4DY
Phone: 020 7406 3333

#372
Cafe Football
Cuisines: Bar, Cafe
Average price: Modest
Area: Stratford, Olympic Village
Address: Westfield Stratford City
London E20 1EN
Phone: 020 8702 2590

#373
Cafe Pacifico
Cuisines: Mexican, Bar
Average price: Modest
Area: Covent Garden
Address: 5 Langley Street
London WC2H 9JA
Phone: 020 7379 7728

#374
Iberica
Cuisines: Tapas, Tapas Bar, Spanish
Average price: Expensive
Area: Westminster
Address: 68 Victoria Street
London SW1E 6SQ
Phone: 020 3327 0200

#375
Souk Medina
Cuisines: Moroccan, Bar, Tea Room
Average price: Modest
Area: Covent Garden
Address: 1a Short's Gardens
London WC2H 9AT
Phone: 020 7240 1796

#376
Polpetto
Cuisines: Italian, Tapas Bar
Average price: Modest
Area: Soho
Address: 11 Berwick Street
London W1F 0PL
Phone: 020 7439 8627

#377
Mint Leaf
Cuisines: Indian, Lounge
Average price: Exclusive
Area: The City
Address: 12 Angel Court
London EC2R 7HB
Phone: 020 7600 0992

#378
La Perla Bar & Grill
Cuisines: Mexican, Tex-Mex, Bar
Average price: Modest
Area: Covent Garden, Strand
Address: 28 Maiden Lane
London WC2E 7JS
Phone: 020 7240 7400

#379
Coppa Club Tower Bridge
Cuisines: Bar, Italian, European
Average price: Modest
Area: Aldgate, The City
Address: 3 Three Quays Walk
London EC3R 6AH
Phone: 020 7993 3827

#380
Bar Gansa
Cuisines: Spanish, Cocktail Bar
Average price: Modest
Area: Camden Town
Address: 2 Inverness Street
London NW1 7HJ
Phone: 020 7267 8909

#381
Balans Soho Society
Cuisines: Breakfast & Brunch,
British, Cocktail Bar
Average price: Modest
Area: Kensington
Address: 187 Kensington High Street
London W8 6SH
Phone: 020 7376 0115

#382
Café Kick
Cuisines: Pub, Coffee & Tea, Tapas
Average price: Modest
Area: Clerkenwell
Address: 43 Exmouth Market
London EC1R 4QL
Phone: 020 7837 8077

#383
Bright Courtyard Club
Cuisines: Cantonese, Dim Sum,
Lounge
Average price: Exclusive
Area: Marylebone
Address: 43-45 Baker St
London W1U 8EW
Phone: 020 7486 6998

#384
The Loop
Cuisines: Bar
Average price: Modest
Area: Mayfair
Address: 19 Dering Street
London W1S 1AH
Phone: 020 7493 1003

#385
Twist At Crawford
Cuisines: Tapas, Tapas Bar,
Breakfast & Brunch
Average price: Expensive
Area: Marylebone
Address: 42 Crawford Street
London W1H 1JW
Phone: 020 7723 3377

#386
Roadhouse Restaurant
Cuisines: Bar, British
Average price: Modest
Area: Covent Garden, Strand
Address: Jubilee Hall 35
London WC2E 8BE
Phone: 020 7240 6001

#387
Taquería
Cuisines: Mexican, Cocktail Bar
Average price: Modest
Area: Notting Hill
Address: 141-145 Westbourne Grove
London W11 2RS
Phone: 020 7229 4734

#388
The Bonneville
Cuisines: Bar, French
Average price: Expensive
Area: Hackney Downs
Address: 43 Lower Clapton Road
London E5 0NS
Phone: 020 8533 3301

#389
Made in Brasil
Cuisines: Brazilian, Bar, Steakhouse
Average price: Modest
Area: Camden Town
Address: 12 Inverness Street
London NW1 7HJ
Phone: 020 7482 0777

#390
Hubbub Cafe Bar
Cuisines: Coffee & Tea,
British, Lounge
Average price: Inexpensive
Area: Isle of Dogs, Millwall
Address: 269 Westferry Road
London E14 3RS
Phone: 020 7515 5577

#391
Prince Regent
Cuisines: Pub, Lounge, British
Average price: Modest
Area: Marylebone
Address: 71 Marylebone High Street
London W1U 5JN
Phone: 020 7486 7395

#392
B Bar
Cuisines: Bar
Average price: Modest
Area: Westminster
Address: 43 Buckingham Palace Road
London SW1W 0PP
Phone: 020 7958 7000

#393
La Barrique Wine Bar
& Restaurant
Cuisines: Pizza, Wine Bar
Average price: Modest
Area: Excel
Address: Warehouse K
ExCel West E16 1DR
Phone: 020 7474 8042

#394
Angels & Gypsies
Cuisines: Spanish, Tapas
Average price: Modest
Area: Camberwell
Address: 29-33 Camberwell Church
Street, London SE5 8TR
Phone: 020 7703 5984

#395
5th View Bar & Food
Cuisines: Tapas Bar, Lounge,
Venue & Event Space
Average price: Modest
Area: St James's
Address: 203-206 Piccadilly
London W1J 9LE
Phone: 020 7851 2433

#396
Las Iguanas
Cuisines: Latin American, Cocktail Bar
Average price: Modest
Area: South Bank, Southwark
Address: Royal Festival Hall Festival
Terrace, London SE1 8XX
Phone: 020 7620 1328

#397
Beach Blanket Babylon
Cuisines: Lounge, European, Buffets
Average price: Expensive
Area: Shoreditch, Bethnal Green
Address: 19-23 Bethnal Green Road
London E1 6LA
Phone: 020 7749 3540

#398
Circus
Cuisines: Asian Fusion,
Cocktail Bar, Cabaret
Average price: Expensive
Area: Covent Garden
Address: 27-29 Endell Street
London WC2H 9BA
Phone: 020 7420 9300

#399
Cafe Koha Bar
Cuisines: European, Bar
Average price: Modest
Area: Covent Garden, Strand
Address: 11 St Martins Court
London WC2N 4AJ
Phone: 020 7497 0282

#400
Señor Ceviche
Cuisines: Cocktail Bar,
Peruvian, Barbeque
Average price: Modest
Area: Soho
Address: Kingly Court
London W1B 5PW
Phone: 020 7842 8540

#401
Hawksmoor Spitalfields Bar
Cuisines: British, Steakhouse, Lounge
Average price: Modest
Area: Spitalfields
Address: 157B Commercial Street
London E1 6BJ
Phone: 020 7426 4856

#402
Zebrano
Cuisines: Bar, European
Average price: Modest
Area: Bloomsbury
Address: 18 Greek Street
London W1D 4DS
Phone: 020 7287 5267

#403
Kiru
Cuisines: Japanese, Cocktail Bar
Average price: Expensive
Area: Chelsea
Address: 2 Elystan Street
London SW3 3NS
Phone: 020 7584 9999

#404
John Salt
Cuisines: American, Bar
Average price: Modest
Area: Angel, Islington
Address: 131 Upper Street
London N1 1QP
Phone: 020 7359 7501

#405
Players Bar and Kitchen
Cuisines: Lounge, British
Average price: Inexpensive
Area: Strand
Address: Villiers Street
London WC2N 6NG
Phone: 020 7930 5868

#406
Belgo Kingsway
Cuisines: Bar, Belgian
Average price: Modest
Area: Covent Garden
Address: 67 Kingsway
London WC2B 6TD
Phone: 020 7242 7469

#407
SkyLounge
Cuisines: Lounge, Cocktail Bar, British
Average price: Expensive
Area: Aldgate, Tower Hill
Address: 7 Pepys Street
London EC3N 4AF
Phone: 020 7709 1043

#408
VOC Grill and Punch House
Cuisines: Bar, Steakhouse
Average price: Modest
Area: King's Cross
Address: 2 Varnishers Yard
London N1 9AW
Phone: 020 7713 8229

#409
Metro Garden Restaurant & Bar
Cuisines: European, Venue & Event
Space, Cocktail Bar
Average price: Expensive
Area: Clapham Common
Address: 9 Clapham Common
Southside, London SW4 7AA
Phone: 020 7627 0632

#410
Kings Road Steakhouse & Grill
Cuisines: British, Steakhouse, Bar
Average price: Exclusive
Area: Chelsea
Address: 386 Kings Road
London SW10 0LR
Phone: 020 7351 9997

#411
Sweetings Restaurant
Cuisines: Fish & Chips, Seafood, Bar
Average price: Expensive
Area: The City
Address: 39 Queen Victoria Street
London EC4N 4SA
Phone: 020 7248 3062

#412
Opium
Cuisines: Dim Sum, Cocktail Bar
Average price: Modest
Area: Chinatown
Address: 15-16 Gerrard Street
London W1D 6JE
Phone: 020 7734 7276

#413
Cafe Sol
Cuisines: Bar, Mexican
Average price: Modest
Area: Clapham, Clapham Common
Address: 56 Clapham High Street
London SW4 7UL
Phone: 020 7498 8558

#414
Goat
Cuisines: Italian, Cocktail Bar
Average price: Expensive
Area: Chelsea
Address: 333 Fulham Road
London SW10 9QL
Phone: 020 7352 1384

#415
Charlotte's Bistro
Cuisines: British, Cocktail Bar,
Breakfast & Brunch
Average price: Expensive
Area: Chiswick
Address: 6 Turnham Green Terrece
London W4 1QP
Phone: 020 8742 3590

#416
Agile Rabbit
Cuisines: Pizza, Bar, Italian
Average price: Inexpensive
Area: Coldharbour Lane/ Herne Hill
Address: Coldharbour Lane
London SW9 8PR
Phone: 020 7998 3448

#417
Rotorino
Cuisines: Italian, Bar
Average price: Modest
Area: Haggerston
Address: 432-434 Kingsland Road
London E8 4AA
Phone: 020 7249 9081

#418
St Clements Café and Bar
Cuisines: Bar, Cafe
Average price: Modest
Area: Holborn
Address: Middle Temple Lane
London EC4Y 9BT
Phone: 020 7936 2755

#419
Beaufort House
Cuisines: Brasserie, Bar
Average price: Modest
Area: Chelsea
Address: 354 Kings Road
London SW3 5UZ
Phone: 020 7352 2828

#420
Dstrkt London
Cuisines: Lounge, European,
Japanese
Average price: Expensive
Area: Leicester Square
Address: 9 Rupert Street
London W1D 6DG
Phone: 020 7317 9120

#421
Checkmate Bar & Restaurant
Cuisines: British, Thai, Bar
Average price: Modest
Area: South Kensington
Address: 117-129 Cromwell Road
London SW7 4DT
Phone: 020 7370 5711

#422
Bar Story
Cuisines: Bar, Pizza
Average price: Modest
Area: Peckham
Address: 213 Blenheim Grove
London SE15 4QL
Phone: 020 7635 6643

#423
Le Paris Grill - Tower Hill
Cuisines: French, Bar, Brasserie
Average price: Expensive
Area: Aldgate
Address: 37 Crutched Friars
London EC3N 2AE
Phone: 020 7680 9999

#424
100 Hoxton
Cuisines: Asian Fusion,
Breakfast & Brunch, Cocktail Bar
Average price: Modest
Area: Hoxton
Address: 100-102 Hoxton Street
London N1 6SG
Phone: 020 7729 1444

#425
Grand Union Brixton
Cuisines: Cocktail Bar, Burgers, Pizza
Average price: Modest
Area: Brixton, Stockwell
Address: 123 Acre Lane
London SW2 5UA
Phone: 020 7274 8794

#426
Copa de Cava
Cuisines: Bar, Spanish
Average price: Modest
Area: Blackfriars
Address: 33 Blackfriars Lane
London EC4V 6EP
Phone: 020 7125 0930

#427
Resident of Paradise Row
Cuisines: Bar, Breakfast & Brunch
Average price: Modest
Area: Bethnal Green
Address: Arch 252 Paradise Row
London E2 9LE
Phone: 020 7729 9609

#428
Union Street Café
Cuisines: Italian, Bar
Average price: Expensive
Area: Southwark
Address: 47-51 Great Suffolk Street
London SE1 0BS
Phone: 020 7592 7977

#429
Artigiano Espresso & Wine Bar
Cuisines: Coffee & Tea, Bar, Cafe
Average price: Inexpensive
Area: Blackfriars
Address: 1 Paternoster Square
St Pauls EC4M 7DX
Phone: 020 7248 0407

#430
Fratelli La Bufala
London Piccadilly
Cuisines: Italian, Pizza, Bar
Average price: Modest
Area: Leicester Square
Address: 40 Shaftesbury Avenue
London W1D 7EY
Phone: 020 7734 3404

#431
Thai Square
Cuisines: Thai, Bar
Average price: Modest
Area: The City
Address: 1-7 Great St Thomas Apostle
London EC4V 2BH
Phone: 020 7329 0001

#432
The Mercer Restaurant & Bar
Cuisines: British, Bar
Average price: Modest
Area: The City
Address: 34 Threadneedle Street
London EC2R 8AY
Phone: 020 7628 0001

#433
Bardens Boudoir
Cuisines: Bar, Cafe
Average price: Inexpensive
Area: Dalston
Address: 36 Stoke Newington Road
London N16 7XJ
Phone: 020 7923 9223

#434
Yates's
Cuisines: Wine Bar, Dance Club, Pub
Average price: Inexpensive
Area: Croydon
Address: 3-11 High Street
Croydon CR0 1QA
Phone: 020 8681 8219

#435
BROWNS
Cuisines: British, Bar, Brasserie
Average price: Expensive
Area: Mayfair
Address: 47 Maddox Street
London W1S 2PG
Phone: 020 7491 4565

#436
Shaws Booksellers
Cuisines: Pub, Cafe
Average price: Modest
Area: Blackfriars
Address: 31-34 ST Andrews Hill
London EC4V 5DE
Phone: 020 7489 7999

#437
Estrela Bar
Cuisines: Bar, Portuguese
Average price: Modest
Area: South Lambeth, Vauxhall
Address: 113 S Lambeth Road
London SW8 1UZ
Phone: 020 7793 1051

#438
Little Italy
Cuisines: Italian, Lounge
Average price: Modest
Area: Bloomsbury
Address: 21 Frith Street
London W1D 4RN
Phone: 020 7734 4737

#439
Made In Camden
Cuisines: Bar, Tapas
Average price: Modest
Area: Camden Town, Chalk Farm
Address: Chalk Farm Rd
London NW1 8EH
Phone: 020 7424 8495

#440
6 St Chad's Place
Cuisines: French, Bar
Average price: Modest
Area: Bloomsbury
Address: 6 St Chad's Place
London WC1X 9HH
Phone: 020 7278 3355

#441
The Cabin Bar & Grill
Cuisines: Lounge, Steakhouse
Average price: Expensive
Area: Chiswick
Address: 148 Chiswick High Road
London W4 1PR
Phone: 020 8994 8594

#442
Tonkotsu Bar & Ramen
Cuisines: Japanese, Bar
Average price: Modest
Area: Soho
Address: 63 Dean Street
London W1D 4QG
Phone: 020 7437 0071

#443
Grand Union Farringdon
Cuisines: Cocktail Bar, Burgers, Pizza
Average price: Modest
Area: Farringdon
Address: 55 Charterhouse Street
London EC1M 6HA
Phone: 020 7251 5259

#444
64th & Social
Cuisines: Steakhouse, Lounge
Average price: Modest
Area: Clapham Common
Address: 64 Clapham High Street
London SW4 7UL
Phone: 020 7627 2535

#445
Kaspar's Seafood Bar and Grill
Cuisines: Seafood, Bar
Average price: Expensive
Area: Strand
Address: The Savoy
London WC2R 0EU
Phone: 020 7420 2111

#446
Bourne & Hollingsworth Buildings
Cuisines: Bar, British, Cafe
Average price: Modest
Area: Clerkenwell
Address: 42 Northampton Road
London EC1R 0HU
Phone: 020 3174 1156

#447
The Bull
Cuisines: Pub, American
Average price: Modest
Area: Highgate
Address: 13 North Hill
London N6 4AB
Phone: 020 8341 0510

#448
Bukowski Grill
Cuisines: Burgers, Bar, American
Average price: Modest
Area: Shoreditch
Address: Bethnal Green Road
London E1 6GY
Phone: 020 7033 6601

#449
Jamon Jamon Soho
Cuisines: Tapas, Spanish, Tapas Bar
Average price: Modest
Area: Bloomsbury
Address: 3-5 Caxton Walk
London WC2H 8PW
Phone: 020 7836 6969

#450
Wedge Issue Pizza
Cuisines: Pizza, Bar
Average price: Modest
Area: Farringdon
Address: 91-95 Clerkenwell Road
London EC1R 5BX
Phone: 020 7242 3246

#451
The Duck and Rice
Cuisines: Chinese, Bar
Average price: Exclusive
Area: Soho
Address: 90 Berwick Street
London W1F 0QB
Phone: 020 3327 7888

#452
Henry's Cafe Bar
Cuisines: British, Bar
Average price: Modest
Area: Mayfair
Address: 80 Piccadilly
London W1J 8HX
Phone: 020 7491 2544

#453
Red Lion
Cuisines: Pub, Cafe
Average price: Inexpensive
Area: Hoxton
Address: 41 Hoxton Street
London N1 6NH
Phone: 020 7837 7816

#454
Jazz Cafe
Cuisines: Bar, British, Music Venue
Average price: Expensive
Area: Camden Town
Address: 5 Parkway
London NW1 7PG
Phone: 020 7688 8899

#455
The Trading House
Cuisines: Cocktail Bar,
Gastropub, Pub
Average price: Modest
Area: The City
Address: 89-91 Gresham Street
London EC2V 7NQ
Phone: 020 7600 5050

#456
The Parlour
Cuisines: Mediterranean,
British, Lounge
Average price: Modest
Area: Canary Wharf, Isle of Dogs
Address: 40 Canada Square Park
London E14 5FW
Phone: 0845 468 0100

#457
Bleeding Heart Tavern
Cuisines: French, Pub
Average price: Expensive
Area: Farringdon
Address: Off Greville Street
London EC1N 8SJ
Phone: 020 7242 8238

#458
Beach Blanket Babylon
Cuisines: Lounge, European,
Cocktail Bar
Average price: Expensive
Area: Notting Hill
Address: 45 Ledbury Road
London W11 2AA
Phone: 020 7229 2907

#459
Salsa!
Cuisines: Dance Club, Tapas Bar,
Latin American
Average price: Inexpensive
Area: Bloomsbury
Address: 96 Charing Cross Road
London WC2H 0JG
Phone: 020 7379 3277

#460
Shotgun
Cuisines: American, Barbeque
Average price: Expensive
Area: Soho
Address: 26 Kingly Street
Soho W1B 5QD
Phone: 020 3137 7252

#461
Pop Art Sushi
Cuisines: Sushi Bar, Italian
Average price: Inexpensive
Area: South Lambeth, Vauxhall
Address: 8 Wandsworth Road
London SW8 2JW
Phone: 020 7582 1114

#462
The Stonhouse
Cuisines: Pub, Cafe
Average price: Modest
Area: Clapham
Address: 165 Stonhouse Street
London SW4 6BJ
Phone: 020 7819 9312

#463
The Fountain Restaurant
Cuisines: American, British
Average price: Expensive
Area: Mayfair
Address: 181 Piccadilly
London W1A 1ER
Phone: 020 7734 8040

#464
Heights Restaurant
Cuisines: British, Cocktail Bar
Average price: Expensive
Area: Soho
Address: 14-15 Langham Place
London W1B 2QS
Phone: 020 7580 0111

#465
Mary Jane's
Cuisines: Lounge, European, Karaoke
Average price: Modest
Area: Aldgate
Address: 124-127 Minories
London EC3N 1NT
Phone: 020 7481 8195

#466
Yates's
Cuisines: Wine Bar, Pub
Average price: Inexpensive
Area: Hounslow
Address: 1-3 Bath Road
Hounslow TW3 3BJ
Phone: 020 8570 0091

#467
Crazy Bear
Cuisines: Thai, Bar
Average price: Expensive
Area: Fitzrovia
Address: 26-28 Whitfield Street
London W1T 2RG
Phone: 020 7631 1188

#468
The Big Chill House
Cuisines: Bar, Burgers, Dance Club
Average price: Modest
Area: Bloomsbury
Address: 257-259 Pentonville Road
London N1 9NL
Phone: 020 7427 2540

#469
Sopranos
Cuisines: Pub, European, Italian
Average price: Modest
Area: Kensington
Address: 183 Kensington High Street
London W8 6SH
Phone: 020 7937 2458

#470
La Brasserie
Cuisines: French, Bar, Tea Room
Average price: Modest
Area: South Kensington
Address: 272 Brompton Road
London SW3 2AW
Phone: 020 7581 3089

#471
B-SOHO Cocktail Bar & Pizzeria
Cuisines: Pizza, Cocktail Bar
Average price: Modest
Area: Soho
Address: 21 Poland Street
London W1F 8QG
Phone: 020 7287 1661

#472
Tiger Tiger
Cuisines: Bar, European
Average price: Modest
Area: Leicester Square
Address: 28-29 Haymarket
London SW1Y 4SP
Phone: 020 7930 1885

#473
The Hideaway
Cuisines: Bar, Pizza, Music Venue
Average price: Inexpensive
Area: Tufnell Park, Upper Holloway
Address: 114 Junction Park Road
London N19 5LB
Phone: 020 7561 0779

#474
Browns
Cuisines: Bar
Average price: Modest
Area: Canary Wharf, Isle of Dogs
Address: Unit A Hertsmere Road West
India Quay, London E14 4AY
Phone: 020 7987 9777

#475
Haunt
Cuisines: British, Bar
Average price: Inexpensive
Area: Stoke Newington Central
Address: 182 Stoke Newington Road
London N16 7UY
Phone: 020 7249 1203

#476
Doost
Cuisines: Persian/Iranian, Bar
Average price: Expensive
Area: Kennington
Address: 305-307 Kennington Road
London SE11 4QE
Phone: 020 7582 3123

#477
Giraffe
Cuisines: American
Average price: Modest
Area: Bloomsbury
Address: 19-21 Brunswick Center
London WC1N 1AF
Phone: 020 7812 1336

#478
The Village
Cuisines: Bar
Average price: Modest
Area: Soho
Address: 81 Wardour Street
London W1D 6QD
Phone: 020 439 4089

#479
North Pole
Cuisines: Bar, European
Average price: Modest
Area: Greenwich
Address: 131 Greenwich High Road
London SE10 8JA
Phone: 020 8853 3020

#480
The Bermondsey Yard
Cuisines: Bar, Cafe
Average price: Modest
Area: Borough
Address: 40 Bermondsey Street
London SE1 3UD
Phone: 020 7378 8978

#481
Zebrano
Cuisines: Bar, Greek
Average price: Modest
Area: Soho
Address: 14 - 16 Ganton Street
London W1F 7BT
Phone: 020 7287 5267

#482
London Grind
Cuisines: Cocktail Bar, Coffee & Tea,
Breakfast & Brunch
Average price: Modest
Area: London Bridge, South Bank
Address: 2 London Bridge
London SW1Y 4UY
Phone: 020 7378 1928

#483
The Alice House
West Hampstead
Cuisines: Breakfast & Brunch,
British, Cocktail Bar
Average price: Modest
Area: Finchley Road, Hampstead
Address: 283-285 West End Lane
London NW6 1RD
Phone: 020 7431 8818

#484
Bavarian Beerhouse
Cuisines: German, Bar
Average price: Modest
Area: Aldgate, Tower Hill
Address: 9 Crutched Friars
London EC3N 2AU
Phone: 0844 330 2005

#485
Smith's Bar & Grill
Cuisines: British, Bar
Average price: Modest
Area: Paddington
Address: 25 Sheldon Square
London W2 6EY
Phone: 020 7286 9458

#486
El Nivel
Cuisines: Bar, Mexican
Average price: Expensive
Area: Covent Garden, Strand
Address: 28 Maiden Lane
London WC2E 7JS
Phone: 020 7240 7400

#487
Sea Containers Restaurant
Cuisines: Seafood, American
Average price: Modest
Area: South Bank, Southwark
Address: 20 Upper Ground
London SE1 9PF
Phone: 020 3747 1063

#488
Hoxley & Porter
Cuisines: Cocktail Bar, British
Average price: Modest
Area: Islington
Address: 153 Upper Street
London N1 1RA
Phone: 020 7226 1375

#489
The Happenstance
Cuisines: Bar, European
Average price: Modest
Area: Blackfriars
Address: 1a Ludgate Hill
London EC4M 7AA
Phone: 0845 468 0104

#490
Que Pasa
Cuisines: Wine Bar
Average price: Modest
Area: Ilford
Address: 108-127 Cranbrook Rd
Ilford IG1 4LZ
Phone: 020 8553 3261

#491
Novikov
Cuisines: Asian Fusion, Italian, Lounge
Average price: Exclusive
Area: Mayfair
Address: 50 Berkeley Street
London W1J 8HA
Phone: 020 7399 4330

#492
The Enterprise Bar
Cuisines: Bar, Gastropub
Average price: Modest
Area: Chelsea
Address: 35 Walton Street
London SW3 2HU
Phone: 020 7584 3148

#493
Bush Hall Dining Rooms
Cuisines: Cocktail Bar, British
Average price: Modest
Area: Shepherd's Bush, White City
Address: 304 Uxbridge Road
London W12 7LJ
Phone: 020 8749 0731

#494
1920
Cuisines: Pool Halls, Burgers,
Cocktail Bar
Average price: Modest
Area: Clerkenwell
Address: 19-20 Great Sutton Street
London EC1V 0DR
Phone: 020 7253 1920

#495
Adventure Bar
Cuisines: Bar, Dance Club
Average price: Modest
Area: Covent Garden, Strand
Address: 20 Bedford Street
London WC2E 9HP
Phone: 020 7924 6055

#496
Lounge
Cuisines: Bar, Breakfast & Brunch
Average price: Modest
Area: Coldharbour Lane/ Herne Hill
Address: 56 Atlantic Road
London SW9 8PY
Phone: 020 7733 5229

#497
Morden & Lea
Cuisines: British, European,
Cocktail Bar
Average price: Modest
Area: Chinatown
Address: 17 Wardour Street
London W1D 6PJ
Phone: 020 3764 2277

#498
Wringer and Mangle
Cuisines: Bar, British
Average price: Modest
Area: London Fields
Address: 13-18 Sidworth Street
London E8 3SD
Phone: 020 3457 7285

#499
Gigalum
Cuisines: Bar, British
Average price: Modest
Area: Clapham Common
Address: 7-8 Cavendish Parade
London SW4 9DW
Phone: 020 8772 0303

#500
Las Iguanas
Cuisines: Latin American, Cocktail Bar
Average price: Modest
Area: Spitalfields
Address: 1 Horner Square
London E1 6AA
Phone: 020 7426 0876

Printed in Great Britain
by Amazon